Irish Hedgerows:
Networks for Nature

Edited and compiled by David Hickie

with contributions from:

Rosaleen Dwyer, Heritage Council representative
Catherine Keena, Teagasc
Frank Macken, Department of Agriculture and Food
Art McCormack, University College Dublin
Brendan McSherry, Heritage Officer
Tom Murphy, Professional Agricultural Contractors (Ireland)

A collaborative venture by *Networks for Nature*

David Hickie qualified from Trinity College, Dublin in environmental sciences in 1985 and has a special interest in trees and forestry. He worked as a professional environmentalist for ten years before becoming a planning and environmental consultant. He is also a writer on Irish and European environmental issues. He lives in Dublin.

Published by Networks for Nature
PO Box 9184, Churchtown, Dublin 14.

Design and layout by Environmental Publications Ltd.

Printed in Ireland

ISBN: 0-9549060-0-4

TABLE OF CONTENTS

NETWORKS FOR NATURE

The maintenance and protection of hedgerows is a responsibility that appears in the remit of a number of government departments, semi-state agencies, non-government organisations, and private and business interests. For all of these stakeholders, hedgerows compete (very often unsuccessfully) with many other pressing concerns for precious time and financial resources.

From the outset, the Networks for Nature initiative was a unique venture. It was designed to act as a forum for all those agencies whose work or livelihood involves or affects hedgerows. Its central objective was to provide a collaborative environment in which to discuss and find practical solutions to some of the issues influencing the long-term management and conservation of Irish hedgerows.

The strength of the project is that it offers a single voice to those principal players whose remit involves or touches upon our hedgerow resource. It draws together government departments, semi-state agencies, farming organisations, environmental concerns, academia, and business interests. The result is a consensus approach, focussing the apparently disparate efforts of these bodies into a single, agreed action.

Represented on the Steering Group who direct Networks for Nature are the project's four funding bodies, the Heritage Council, the Department of Agriculture and Food, the National Parks and Wildlife Service of the Department of Environment, Heritage and Local Government, and the Forest Service. Also represented on the Steering Group are Teagasc, the Irish Farmers' Association, Local Authority Heritage Officers, the Professional Agricultural Contractors of Ireland, and University College Dublin. Representatives from environmental organisations have also made welcome contributions to the project.

The production of a book on Irish hedgerows was afforded a high priority during the early days of the Networks for Nature project. Indeed, the sources of information were sitting around the table! The many contributions to the text have been skilfully drawn together, edited, and added to by David Hickie. The result is a work that will appeal to a wide range of interests.

The publication of this long overdue book represents a consensus approach of all involved, holding true to Networks for Nature's mission statement, 'Conservation through Collaboration'.

Dr. Rosaleen Dwyer,
Chairman of Steering Group,
Networks for Nature,
October 2004

FOREWORD

Have you ever cut a fishing pole from a hedgerow hazel, picked cowslips or violets on a Sunday walk? Perhaps! Or used the tight flower buds of whitethorn as ammunition for your peashooter that you contrived from the hollow stem of cow parsley growing nearby? Did you eat the fresh leaves in April and call them "Cheese and Onion", or nibble the ripe, mushy haws in autumn? Have you ever defied the thorns to catch a glimpse of the gaping fledglings in a finch's nest? Has the casual sight of a hedgerow shrub vibrating with bees or the fleeting beauty of a proud cowering clump of primroses ever evoked in you thoughts of the bitter-sweet reality of our own tenuous existence?

Hedgerows are redolent of county youthful days, bygone summers when the sun shone high in the sky, the hay was always saved and all was well with the world. Perhaps we worked with our parents, brothers and sisters in summer meadows, rushing to take porous shelter under the dripping hedgerow canopy when the sky opened. Who among us has memories of going with their fathers to "stick a bush in a gap" where the stock had broken out? Good fences make good neighbours! In late summer, we picked blackberries from fierce briars with stained fingers. We ate sloes, relishing the soft flesh, already anticipating the bitter disappointment of the sand-dry mouth vermouth. We wondered at the blue bloom on the skin; plum-like, promising so much, delivering so little.

For urban dwellers too, hedgerows are evocative of carefree schooldays – a caravel, crewed with rowdy, excited kids and motley dogs – tramping around the headlands of early spring fields with wet shoes, looking for birds nests with destruction on your minds: magpies beware! or cursing your luck when your only plastic football became impaled at the top of that treacherous bush under the lamp at the end of your street. Many's a whitethorn that's hoarded grudgingly in its branches the detritus of the locality: stones. bottles, tin cans deposited by errant children with time on their hands. Whitethorn has this capacity to covet anything that is thrown into its arms. For many of us the waltz has continued into adulthood.

The annual flowering of hedgerow shrubs, in particular the whitethorn, is a much anticipated feast for the senses and a potent reminder that summer is just around the corner. No matter how cavalier our attitude to hedgerows, they cannot be ignored at this time of year. They jump out at us from every quarter, demanding our attention. Visitors to Ireland are constantly enraptured by such an outburst of colour – a veritable botanic gardens in our backyard. Hedgerows often provide us with the only tangible link between town and country, a neutral ground where understanding and sympathy can be exercised for the townie and culchie alike.

In general, we are positively disposed to hedgerows, if often somewhat ambivalent in our attitude. We are conscious of their presence. Hedgerows count down the year like any calendar, and reflect nature's ever-changing moods. They delineate the landscape and carve it up into appreciable portions, which seem to provide us with the assurance that we are in control. Great expanses of open landscape, while evoking a genuine sense of wonder, often raise in us a little panic. There is comfort in a hedged landscape.

The key to understanding the Irish landscape – and ourselves for that matter – lies in the distant past. All around us – those sturdy field walls and hedged banks which we so readily identify as giving such character to the Irish countryside are by no means as immutable as they first appear. They are of our own creation and the pattern they make has changed over the centuries in response to our needs.

Hedgerows evoke history and folklore: references to the Táin, booleying of cattle, estates, evil landlords, hedge schools, fairy and mile bushes and a famine peasant population housed against their banks, sheltering in hovels constructed from the very sods of the land that had forsaken them. Is it any wonder that at times we are desensitised to their plight?

Agriculture has, from the very outset, used hedgerows to contain and demarcate its various activities. Hedgerows, walls and earth banks, the fruits of great physical effort and toil, permit herding of farmed animals and delineate ownership. Our pastoral ancestors required to contain their animals and protect their crops from damage and predation. A thick, thorny hedge will equally serve the same purpose today. The wolves may have changed their clothing but the dangers persist. Concern is often voiced about the long-term future of our hedgerows. They are as secure or insecure as our own existence – it's a matter of perception and whether we have the confidence in a future that extends beyond our own life span. It requires us to adopt a modicum of altruism and cooperation. A positive attitude towards our visual landscape is in essence giving life to our dreams of a better world. The responsibility rests with us all. Us? Yes – you and me! We need to act for the common good and future generations.

In the last thirty years, we have moved from an agriculturally-based society to a modern manufacturing and service economy. Our population is mobile and dispersed throughout the country. Many of us are not actively involved in agriculture and view the land from a very different perspective. Society is seeking to allocate more weight to the ecological and aesthetic values of our landscape. When we reassign new values to any asset – and surely our hedgerows are an asset of national import – we need to re-assess and devise a sensitive policy for its continued survival. This is the crux of the issue.

It is timely and opportune to look again at our hedgerows and decide how best to treat them. This book has embraced the topic of Irish hedgerows with enthusiasm and offers an agreed approach to enable us all to appreciate and enjoy this unique feature of our landscape.

Frank Macken, November 2004

CHAPTER 1. HEDGEROWS IN THE MAKING

The hedged landscape from the air. Hedgerows connect with patches of woodland. Note the many hedgerow trees. (Photo: Con O'Rourke)

Setting the scene

Hedgerows are such a familiar part of the rural scene that we have tended to take them for granted. Practically every field on low ground has a hedgerow around it. Yet, this patchwork quilt landscape of fields bordered by hedgerows is very unusual in Europe. Britain is the only other country that has an extensive hedgerow network. Elsewhere in Europe, hedgerow landscapes are still found in Brittany and Normandy (known as 'bocage'), northern Italy, Greece and the Austrian Alps, but they find their best expression in Ireland.

Hedgerows are woodlands in miniature, and both these habitats have many species of trees, plants and animals in common. A single hedgerow, viewed on its own perhaps might not amount to much. Yet collectively, hedgerows dress what would otherwise be a bleak landscape and give rural Ireland a comfortably wooded feel. They form a complex network connecting farm with farm, townland with townland, habitat with habitat. They occupy an area larger than that of all our broadleaf woodlands put together, and hold fifteen per cent of Ireland's stock of broadleaf trees.

The first hedgerows

Many hedgerows are not very old. Most were planted from the mid-1700s up to the mid-1800s. But woven through this more modern landscape tapestry are older hedgerows which date from Gaelic Ireland, in the age before colonisation by England. They would have developed on top of banks which were dug to mark townland boundaries. Hedgerows were not just used for farming. They were also planted on top of earth banks, such as raths, to provide an additional barrier to hostile forces. Medieval historian Harry Long describes one such example:

"Hedges planted on top of earthen banks increased the defensive capabilities of a settlement, and were used as such in raths. As late as 1600, the rath at Tullahogue in Hugh O'Neill's country was still occupied and a contemporary picture shows the trees growing from an encircling bank."

(Photo: David Hickie)

These old hedgerows sometimes survive to this day — venerable reminders of an older culture which could not withstand the modernising forces of the colonial power.

The tree laws and mythology of ancient Ireland

According to John Feehan in his book *Farming in Ireland*, living hedgerows were not specifically referred to in the Brehon Laws of Gaelic Ireland. Four types of field boundaries were recognised: drystone walls, bank and ditch, wickerwork fence and oak fence. Drystone walls, banks and ditches are still with us today, and have often become hedgerows simply because trees and bushes have taken root there.

Hedgerows also developed around enclosed woodland and from remnants of woodland which were progressively cut back to a point where they became merely a linear strip — a practice called assarting.

In Gaelic Ireland, hedgerows were indeed treated as woodland strips and supplied wood for a variety of uses. In the Brehon Laws, trees were classified into four classes according to their uses. The chieftain trees were oak, hazel, holly, yew, ash, pine and apple. The peasant trees were alder, willow, whitethorn, rowan, birch and elm. The shrub trees were blackthorn, elder, aspen and juniper. The bramble trees included dog-rose, bramble, heather, ivy and gorse. As we shall see in later chapters, most of these trees can be found in hedgerows.

In Gaelic Ireland, people possessed a special affinity for nature which has atrophied over the centuries. Myth and magic were associated with nature and especially with trees. The whitethorn, the mainstay of our hedgerows, was associated with spring and marriage. The month of May, when the whitethorns blossom, was a traditionally a time of joyous celebration. Whitethorn was widely regarded as a sacred tree in ancient times and, even to this day, it is considered unlucky to cut down the 'lone thorn' or sceach. The magic and legends associated with whitethorn are found in Britain too, since they shared the same Celtic tradition, grounded on an intimacy with the spirits of Nature. Even today, as the whitethorn blossom droops in white cascades, it gives us a timeless sign that the cloak of winter has finally been thrown off and summer has arrived.

The coming of the whitethorn brings on earth heaven,
All the spring speaks out in one sweet word,
And heaven grows gladder, knowing that earth has heard.
Swinburne

The hazel, also found widely in hedgerows, was regarded as the tree of knowledge and the nuts were especially sought after as the repository of ancient wisdom. Holly protected people during the dark winter months, while crab apple was symbolic of the giving of love. Elder is also known as the 'bore tree' or 'bour tree' in parts of Ulster and Scotland, originating from the use of hollowed-out elder branches as pipes for blowing air onto fires.

The folklore and mythology surrounding trees developed in an age where people were much closer to nature than we are. Although we have become detached and insulated from the natural world, there is a renewed interest in the folklore and mythology of trees. This subject merits a book in itself, and readers are

HAZEL
Regarded as the tree of knowledge.

ELDER
Also known as the Bore tree.

(Photo: Catherine Keena)

directed to *Irish Trees: Myths, Legends and Folklore* by Niall Mac Coitir (see Bibliography).

The foundations of the hedged landscape

Imagine being transported back to rural Ireland in the 1700s. What would it look like? We can get some idea by reading Dr. Arthur Young's "Tour of Ireland". Young was a progressive English agriculturalist, who commented in detail on his tour of Ireland between 1776 and 1779. For example, he wrote:

"...in a word, the greatest part of the kingdom exhibits a naked, bleak, dreary view for want of wood, which has been destroyed for a century past, with the most thoughtless prodigality, and still continues to be cut and wasted."

Yet Young was also unconvinced by the claims of some landowners that their tenants were responsible for this waste, and he laid the blame squarely at the feet of the landowners. He also observed that a number of progressive landowners were planting trees, fencing their properties and creating fields as we know them today. The fences they used were hedgerows — living fences — which marked out property boundaries and made fields which controlled the movement of livestock. Before this, most holdings were open and unfenced. This systematic partitioning of land into discrete farm holdings was called 'enclosure'. The hedged landscape was fashioned slowly but systematically on a grand scale and for a purpose, as we shall see below.

"Enclosure of the land was inspired by the Agricultural Revolution"

The enclosure of the land in Ireland was inspired by the Agricultural Revolution which had already begun in England. New arable farming techniques and selective breeding of livestock could increase yields dramatically, but they could not be used in the open field system and shared, communal grazing land that was the norm at the time. Enclosure also made it easier for land to be reclaimed, in the same way that land reclamation often followed division of commonages in 20th century Ireland.

Landowners in 18th century Ireland were obliged by law to erect fences, as in England. An Act of Parliament which promoted enclosure was passed in 1697. This Act obliged landowners to erect proper permanent boundaries between their properties, and was followed by a further Act in 1721 which gave specifications for many of the boundary ditches and hedgerows which still exist today.

"Enclosure was often unpopular with smaller tenant farmers..."

Enclosure of land was very expensive and was of most benefit to larger landowners, allowing them to consolidate their holdings. In both Ireland and England, enclosure was often unpopular with smaller tenant farmers because it deprived them of the use of common land on which they had traditional grazing rights. Rural protest movements were a common reaction to laws imposed on tenants, including enclosure. Our romantic ideas about hedgerows might be tempered by the fact that enclosure increased poverty among the landless rural people. Eighteenth century Ireland was a harsh place for tenant farmers. Many lived in grinding poverty — even worse than their English counterparts — and were forced to pay extortionate rents. And they had to maintain their fences. From the mid-1600s onwards, there are increasing numbers of leases binding tenant farmers to make whitethorn hedges and plant and maintain trees within them.

The following poem probably dates from the 18th century. It is a protest against the enclosure movement in England. Many rural people of the time believed that the parliamentary enclosures were 'official theft' of common land.

The law demands that we atone
When we take things we do not own
But leaves the lords and ladies fine
Who take things that are yours and mine.

The poor and wretched don't escape
If they conspire the law to break;
This must be so but they endure
Those who conspire to make the law.

The law locks up the man or woman
Who steals the goose from off the common
And geese will still a common lack
Till they go and steal it back.

                    Anonymous, no date.

11

"The new planters brought with them the customs of their own country"

John Feehan describes, in his book *Farming in Ireland*, the progress of enclosure which followed in the wake of the English plantations from the late 1600s onwards. The new planters brought with them the customs of their own country. The Archdeacon of Meath, John Bramhall remarked that you could tell if an area had been planted with English "from the hedges and other badges".

The progress of enclosure

The progress of enclosure around the country was uneven. In counties such as Laois and Westmeath, fencing and ditching was less in evidence than in Dublin, Kildare, Meath and Louth. Samuel Lewis in 1837 wrote of Co. Louth: "The fences are generally quickset hedges, although the broad bank of earth or sods and the dry stonewall are to be met with in some parts". And the style of enclosure varied according to the region. So, for instance in North Leinster, the hedges were whitethorn, while in south Leinster and east Munster, enclosure was by means of banks planted with gorse. The stone-faced banks of Wexford belonged to a style unique to that county; and large double ditches were the fashion in the east of the country around 1730-40. Most of the hedgerows bounding large rectangular fields in Leinster and on better farmland elsewhere were planted from 1740 to 1830.

Usually enclosure progressed most rapidly on the better farmland in the east, which was by then owned mainly by English planter stock. John Feehan notes that hedgerows in the modern sense were virtually unknown until

(Photo: David Hickie)

the progressive new agriculture in England reached us in the early 1800s. Samuel Lewis described the situation in Co. Kilkenny in the 1830s:

"The fences generally are very indifferent, principally consisting of an old broad mound of earth (called a ditch), with a deep and broad trench on one or both sides, or of dry and broken stone walls, except in the immediate neighborhood of Kilkenny or on the farms of gentlemen, where in many instances quickset hedges show to great advantage:"

(Photo: David Hickie)

Outside Leinster, small regular fields were made on good farmland, while small irregular fields are more typical of more marginal land, especially in the west. West of the Shannon, only some of the larger estates underwent enclosure. Arthur Young described one example in detail when he visited Strokestown Park in Co. Roscommon:

"His hedgerows Mr Mahon (the owner) has planted with uncommon attention, the ditches are single, with a row of trees among or above the quick, another row on the back of the bank, and a third on the brow of the ditch; these, with a lofty growth of the quick, forms so thick a shelter, that one cannot see through it, so that almost every enclosure has the appearance of field, surrounded by a wood."

The political stability of the 18th and early 19th centuries allowed agriculture to develop rapidly. This was an expansive age. In parallel, the road network was also being modernised, and indeed Arthur Young remarked that some of the Irish roads were in better condition than their equivalents in England. Roadside hedgerows were originally planted from the late 1700s to the early 1800s, when the foundations for our contemporary road layout were made. The predecessors of our county councils, the Grand Juries, made orders for most of these hedgerows to be planted.

Tenant farmers inherit the land

The devastation of the Famine overshadowed almost everything else in the 1840s. After the Famine, the optimistic era of tree planting and hedging had ended. Economic and political circumstances changed, and the Irish land-owning class found itself lacking in support from Britain which, by the latter part of the 1800s was going through a period of enlightenment and reform. The writing was on the wall for the large estates. Most did not survive intact into the 1900s, and many of the remaining woodlands were ransacked for their remaining good timber. In 1870, nearly 10% of Ireland was owned by just 20 people. After the passing of the first Land Act, only 3% of Irish householders owned any land. But by 1916, it had risen to 63.9%. In the space of half a century, Ireland had undergone a social revolution.

At Independence in 1922, Ireland had been virtually stripped of trees, and only about 54,000 ha (130,000 acres) of woodland survived. However, many hedgerows did survive in an otherwise treeless landscape. They became the fences and boundaries of a new breed of landowners, many of whose forebears had been tenant farmers.

Enclosure was a very gradual process, taking hundreds of years; nevertheless it transformed the rural landscape. This change would have been even more extensive and striking than that brought about by the expansion of plantation forestry in our own time.

(Photo: David Hick·

CHAPTER 2. THE MODERN RURAL LANDSCAPE

Bringing in the harvest in one large field surrounded by tightly trimmed hedgerows. Hedgerows have tended to be removed on intensive tillage farms. (Photo: Con O'Rourke)

The hedged landscape we see today is a creation of several centuries past, which suited the agriculture and the political situation of its time. But farming has changed dramatically since then. Machines do the work that horses and men once did. Farm labour has shrunk to a tiny fraction of that which it once was. Agricultural contractors sow and harvest crops with large, powerful machines, sometimes through the night. Isn't it remarkable that the hedged landscape has survived at all, despite being created in an age of horse power and abundant, cheap labour?

The main reason hedgerows have survived is that Irish agriculture is dominated by grass-based livestock farming. Tillage (such as cereals, rape and sugar beet) accounts for about nine per cent of the total agricultural area, whereas in most other EU countries, this figure is much higher. Since hedgerows are less important now as fences, they have tended to be forgotten and left to one side; or they have been trimmed unsympathetically, reducing their vigour and their attractiveness for wildlife.

Large, regular fields bounded by hedgerows – typical of intensively farmed land in the east of Ireland (Photo: Con O'Rourke)

The advent of wire fencing made the maintenance of hedgerows for stock control less relevant. However, hedgerows reduce nose to nose contact between herds and help reduce the spread of disease. Hedgerows make good property boundaries, and give shelter and warmth to livestock and people alike.

Hedgerows were removed from tillage areas from the 1960s onwards. Fields were too small for large, modern farm machinery. Once this movement gathered momentum, it was hard to stop. As much as one quarter of all hedgerows in Britain has been removed since the Second World War. In the 1980s, realising that some of this removal was unnecessary, the British government turned towards encouraging the conservation and re-planting of hedgerows. Now, in the early years of the 21st century, farmers have less incentive to remove them.

European agricultural policy re-models rural Ireland's landscape

Since we joined the then EEC in 1973, the CAP has helped to re-model the rural landscape. Until the early 1990s, if farmers produced more, they were paid more. The EU supported prices of milk, beef, cereals and sugar beet, and there were generous grants for farm buildings, land reclamation and drainage. The old ways of farming, in slow retreat for decades, disappeared rapidly. Rivers were canalised, wetlands drained and scrub, woodland and hedgerows removed, all paid for by grant-aided schemes.

A new road taking shape. A section of hedgerow has been removed. (Photo: David Hickie)

We do not know exactly how many hedgerows were removed (since there were no countrywide surveys), but it appears that the loss was less than in other EU countries. A few small scale studies give us some idea of hedgerow losses. In North County Dublin, for example, 16 per cent of hedgerows were removed from 1937 to 1984. In Co. Cavan, a survey of 20 farms revealed an average removal rate of 18 per cent from 1908 to the mid-1990s. A survey of progressive farmers in Cavan showed that 31 per cent of hedgerows were removed in the same period (Keena, 1998). Removal of hedgerows in very small fields allowed more efficient farming, contributing to a viable agricultural industry.

The CAP has changed over time because of agricultural surpluses and societal demands. Now, there are fewer incentives to produce more crops and livestock, and more emphasis is placed on environmental management.

The first national farming and environmental scheme

Farmers had to adjust quickly to this shift in policy. In 1994, while the Farm Improvement Programme still supported land reclamation, the Rural Environment Protection Scheme (REPS) was launched, one of the main aims of which is to protect and manage hedgerows. Under this EU and nationally co-funded voluntary scheme, farmers agree to undertake actions to conserve the landscape and nature on their farms.

The current REPS is available to in excess of seventy per cent of Irish farmers. While the scheme is not attractive to most intensive farmers, there is scope within the agri-environmental programme to facilitate this sector in the future. This will provide the opportunity to protect the hedgerows of the countryside.

Hedgerows are lost through neglect as well as removal

Some hedgerows are dying out slowly due to neglect. With the advent of wire, farmers have found it hard to justify the labour and expense of maintaining them. Neglect usually shows up as gaps in the hedgerow, where hedging shrubs and trees have died. The experienced eye can see that a fair proportion of our hedgerows have poor vigour. This is to be expected, since whitethorn and other species have a limited life span. We can't yet put a figure on the proportion of Irish hedgerows in poor condition, but in Britain, it has been estimated that more than seven times more hedgerows have been lost from neglect rather than removal. The current REPS gives farmers the option of planting new hedgerows and improving and extending the life of existing hedgerows. These techniques are explained in Chapter 5.

Hedgerows – devoured by the Celtic Tiger?

In the land of the Celtic Tiger, hedgerows are more likely to be removed by builders and local authorities than farmers. We are living in a time of unprecedented building development. Within one generation, emigration has become a thing of the past and more people want to stay and live in rural Ireland. Every small town is expanding to meet the demand of people moving out from the major cities or returning from abroad.

Tall, mature whitethorn hedgerows in May, Co. Kilkenny. (Photo: Catherine Keena)

Land values have soared, and new house building has mushroomed. Hedgerows are swept away as housing estates on the outskirts of towns swallow up farmland, and new designs have, up to now, rarely included the retention of hedgerows. This trend is changing as a few enlightened local authorities are specifically requiring hedgerows to be retained in housing developments.

When one-off houses are built in rural areas, local authorities often require the boundary with the road to be moved back several metres to allow for possible future road widening. Up until recently, this has usually meant that a section of hedgerow is removed permanently. Again, this is changing gradually, as local authorities adopt more enlightened policies (see Chapter 6 and Appendix 2).

Every new road that slices through the countryside sweeps away any hedgerows that lie in its path. Trimming in summer when birds are nesting is a major issue.

Protecting, maintaining and improving this vast network of bushy fences may seem a daunting task, but in fact we can make substantial progress by improving the approach, techniques and timing of hedgerow maintenance.

Opportunities for the future

We are presented with more challenging tasks if we want to protect hedgerows of special ecological or historical value, extend the life of old hedgerows or plant new hedgerows. Nevertheless, the techniques are well-established and good advice is available. There has never been a better time than the present to meet these challenges.

Guelder rose in a new roadside
hedgerow, Co. Monaghan
(Photo: David Hickie)

A heavy crop of elderberries –
valuable food for birds in autumn.
(Photo: David Hickie)

Chapter 3. The nature of hedgerows

"Hedgerows can support an astonishing variety of wild plants and animals"

The natural beauty of the Irish countryside reveals itself in spring. The hedgerows come to life once more after their long winter sleep. A myriad of creatures which live in and around hedgerows, large and small, begin to wake up in tune with the hedgerows' annual cycle. Considering their small size, hedgerows support an astonishing variety of wild plants and animals. It is estimated that over 600 of Ireland's 815 species of flowering plants live in hedgerows. The Irish Wildlife Federation recorded 37 species of shrubs and trees and 105 species of wild flora in hedgerows.

Hedgerows teem with life. Their flora provide pollen and nectar for a myriad of insects. When autumn comes, hedgerows provide a bountiful larder of fruit, nuts and berries for wild birds, mammals and a host of other small creatures. The tangle of branches is ideal for nesting birds. Grasses and other plants along the base and margins give cover for small mammals such as wood mice and pygmy shrews and food and cover for a host of invertebrates.

Associated drains can harbour various water plants, aquatic invertebrates and frogs. A hedge bank offers sites for badger setts and fox earths. Holes in old hedgerow trees can provide homes for bats and birds such as the Barn Owl.

The natural history of hedgerows

The ecology of a typical hedgerow is best explained by looking first at its structure, in other words, the various parts that make it up. At the bottom, there is often an earth bank on which the shrubs and trees have been planted or have self-seeded. The bank will tend to vary in size and shape depending on the county or region. The hedge bank would have been built up from earth removed from an adjacent drain, which may or may not carry water. Alongside the bank and drain is a grassy margin or, alongside the road, a verge, which can vary in width depending on how the field is managed. The margin is usually uncultivated.

Growing on top of the bank are shrubs which make up the main body of the hedgerow and which would have been planted with the aim of making a stockproof fence. Over the years, planted shrubs would have been supplemented by species which have colonised naturally. In amongst the hedging plants are taller trees, which were either planted or have self-seeded.

The bank

Fox earths, badger setts and rabbit burrows are often found in the hedge bank. Ireland's only native reptile, the Common Lizard, can be found on dry hedgerow banks. The faces of shady hedge banks are ideal for primroses, foxgloves and the cuckoo pint, which emerge in spring. Ferns and mosses like the damp and shady environment that the bank provides.

THE DRAIN

The drain may act as a field drain which could be dry except during rainy periods, or it could have a permanent stream flowing through it. Plants which like damp places can be found here, such as mosses and liverworts, watercress, water mint, marsh cinquefoil, brooklime and bur-marigold. Frogs and newts spawn in water-filled drains, which are also a habitat for aquatic invertebrates.

THE MARGIN

The hedgerow margin is a strip of uncultivated, grassy vegetation adjoining the base, which can be rich in flowering plants if protected from excessive grazing, fertiliser, slurry or pesticides. This grassy strip is very important for the wildlife potential of a hedgerow.

One of the most visible flowering plants, especially on roadside verges in spring, is cow parsley. In the same family are hogweed and wild angelica and the introduced alexanders, which tower above the grasses in the spring and summer. These grass and broadleaved plant species are not found on intensively managed land. They support a wide range of wildlife. Nettles, for example, are the food plant for caterpillars of the three colourful butterflies: the Small Tortoiseshell, Peacock and Red Admiral, while grasses support the caterpillars of the Meadow Brown and Speckled Wood. Seed eating birds such as Goldfinch and Linnet feed on small seeds. Hedgerows can harbour certain insect pests, but also their predators. For example, lacewings and hoverfly larvae play their part in controlling aphid infestations in crops.

Hedgerows are networks for nature within the farmed landscape. (Photo: Catherine Keena)

Ideally, the wild margin or roadside verge should be as wide as is practicable.

Hedgerow species

Shrubs comprise the main body of the hedgerow. The best times to identify the different species are either in the spring, when they are in flower, or in the autumn, when the fruits ripen.

Whitethorn (*Crataegus monogyna*), also called hawthorn, is by far the most common shrub. Its thorns deter stock and it tolerates routine trimming. Its creamy blossom transforms the rural landscape in May, and is an abundant source of nectar for bees. The berries (haws) are eaten by birds and field mice in winter.

Only one species is native in Ireland, whereas in Britain, it is accompanied by the Midland thorn (*Crataegus laevigata*).

The blossom of the blackthorn (*Prunus spinosa*), emerging before the leaves, is often the first hedgerow shrub to be noticed in spring. When well-established, its sharp thorns make it an impenetrable barrier. The dark blue fruits, called sloes, ripen in late autumn and are eaten by birds and used for wines and sloe gin. Blackthorn is the food plant of no fewer than 200 species of moths.

Crab apple (*Malus sylvestris*), wild cherry (*Prunus avium*) and wild pear (*Pyrus pyraster*) are less common blossom-forming trees of

Hedgerow blossoms.

Blackthorn blossoms emerge before the leaves in early spring. (D. Hickie)

Whitethorn, whose leaves emerge before flowering in May. (C. Keena)

Elder blossom in summer. (D. Hickie)

Crab apple in blossom in a relict hedgerow. (C. Keena)

hedgerows which add to the harvest of fruit in the hedgerows in autumn. Genuine wild crab apples are hard to find, as they have hybridised with orchard cultivars for generations. Native wild pears are much less common.

Bramble (*Rubus fruticosus agg.*) and dog rose (*Rosa canina*) are widespread, thorny hedgerow shrubs which provide abundant nectar and fruit for animals which live in and visit the hedgerows. Bramble is an early coloniser of hedgerows, while dog rose is often associated with those long-established.

Elder (*Sambucus niger*) is a very common coloniser of hedgerows but was never deliberately planted. Elder in a stockproof hedgerow is viewed as undesirable by some: it grows quickly through the hedge but when it dies, it leaves a gap. However, elder blossom and elderberries are wonderful food sources for wildlife. Elder is often associated with old dwellings, and sometimes with badger setts. Wine is made from elder flowers and berries.

Hazel (*Corylus avellana*) is an understorey tree of native woodland, preferring drier, more fertile ground. Hazel could have been planted in some hedgerows, but otherwise it is a slow coloniser. Hazel is often found in townland boundary and other older hedgerow banks. Catkins emerge in February and are very distinctive when nothing else is in leaf. Hazel

Hedgerow fruits

Whitethorn (D. Hickie)

Blackthorn (D. Hickie)

Crab apple (C. Keena)

Dog rose (D. Hickie)

nuts ripen in late autumn, and are eaten by field mice, squirrels and children.

Gorse (*Ulex europaeus*), also called furze and whin is very common in hedgerows in some parts of the country, notably Counties Wicklow and Wexford. Gorse does colonise hedgerows naturally, but was originally planted on some hedge banks, notably in the south-east. In the past it was fed to stock.

Holly (*Ilex aquifolium*) is another tree of the understorey of native woodland and often found in older hedgerows. The red berries of the female tree are popular for Christmas decorations but in some counties, such as Kerry, they have been overexploited.

Ivy (*Hedera helix*) is ubiquitous as a hedgerow shrub and, while not a parasite, a heavy growth of ivy will tend to make trees more vulnerable to being blown down in storms. However, ivy provides food and cover for insects and birds.

Other common native climbers include old man's beard (*Clematis vitalba*) and honeysuckle (*Lonicera periclymenum*).

Elms (usually *Ulmus glabra*) are still present in hedgerows around the country, but nearly always as shrubs — mature elms have been all but wiped out by Dutch Elm Disease.

Hedgerow fruits.

Elder (*D. Hickie*)

Bramble (*D. Hickie*)

Guelder Rose (*C. Keena*)

Buckthorn (*D. Hickie*)

27

Spindle (*Euonymus europaeus*) also called pegwood, was so named because its hard wood was used for making spindles and skewers. It can be found in hedgerows in limestone areas, such as the Midlands. Spindle is especially distinctive when the rose-pink berries — called 'cardinals' hats' — mature in autumn, and survive long after the leaves have fallen.

Guelder Rose (*Viburnum opulus*), like the spindle, is another striking shrub that appears to go unnoticed in our hedgerows. It is not a rose but belongs to the same family as elder and honeysuckle. The flowers are a disc of creamy blossoms which produce translucent red fruit in early autumn. Guelder rose thrives on damp soils, often near a drain.

Lilac (*Syringa vulgaris*), with its heavily scented flowers, has escaped from gardens and can occasionally be found in hedgerows, along with wild privet (*Ligustrum vulgare*) and dogwood (*Cornus sanguinea*), with its very characteristic red stems in winter. In damp areas, such as alongside waterways, willows (*Salix* species) and alder (*Alnus glutinosa*) will tend to dominate hedgerows.

Fuchsia hedges are common in parts of the west and south-west, especially Co. Kerry. *Fuchsia magellanica* comes originally from Chile and Argentina but the species we are familiar with is a cultivated variety, introduced here in the late 1700s.

Hedgerow trees

Hedgerow trees are one of the great scenic assets of the lowland rural landscape, giving it the appearance of being comfortably wooded.

Above: dead elm and below, leaves on a healthy, young elm. (Photos: David Hickie)

Quite apart from their landscape value, they are also extremely valuable for wildlife. Leases from the 1600s and laws from the 1700s required the planting of trees in hedgerows. The graceful old oak, beech and ash which cast their proud crowns over the hedgerows of well-managed farms were probably planted for timber. However, ash will colonise hedgerows and many ash trees will have self-seeded. Nearly 80 per cent of ash for hurleys is imported each year because so little good ash timber is grown here. Topping of ash produces multi-stems which are useless for hurleys.

Some facts on the wildlife value of hedgerows

Of the 110 bird species regularly recorded in the Countryside Bird Survey in Ireland during the breeding season, 55 use hedgerows. Of these, 35 nest in hedgerows over 1.4 metres high and 1.3 metres wide, which provide cover from overhead and ground predators.

A survey of 153 hedgerows in counties Offaly and Wexford found a strong positive relationship between bird species richness and hedgerow size, particularly area and the number of trees present in the hedgerow. The presence of a drain and hedge margin width were also important for birds. Structurally diverse hedges held more bird species. The commonest birds recorded were Wren, Robin, Blackbird, Chaffinch, Dunnock and Song Thrush. Goldcrest was also quite abundant in hedgerows (in contrast to the UK). The more common species were similar in terms of their hedgerow associations. However, a number of species, including Dunnock and Yellowhammer, were more associated with lower hedgerows with fewer trees. (Flynn, 2002)

The stark, bleached tree skeletons in hedgerows are often dead elms, killed by the fungus, Dutch Elm Disease. The fungus, and the beetle that carries it from tree to tree, may die down to a point where the disease is no longer a threat.

Of the trees which have become 'naturalised' in Ireland, sycamore (*Acer pseudoplatanus*), beech (*Fagus sylvatica*) and horse chestnut (*Aesculus hippocastanum*) are common in hedgerows, especially along roadsides.

Mature hedgerow trees offer opportunities for wildlife and are ecosystems in themselves. Branches of high trees provide perches for birds of prey, Wood Pigeons and various members of the crow family. Oak supports 284 species of insects and mites, while willow supports 266.

Contrary to what you might think, overmature and dead trees are also extremely important for wildlife, since they provide homes for a host of invertebrate species which will not normally occur on well-manicured farms. Dead and dying trees provide nesting space for birds such as the Barn Owl, various members of the tit family and roosting areas for bats, all of which are protected species. These old trees will eventually decay and will need to be replaced. This is one reason why it is important to allow some trees to 'escape' from the hedgerow and grow to their full height.

How hedgerow management affects wildlife

Hedgerows were originally planted as stockproof fences, now supplemented by the addition of barbed wire and electric fences. They were originally cut manually, but are now normally cut mechanically using the flail or circular saw (see Chapter 5). While many hedgerows are trimmed periodically, some are not managed at all. This is not necessarily a bad thing. Traditionally, the landscape of rural Ireland was never 'manicured', like some other countries. Some venerable old hedgerows are best left alone to grow wild and unkempt, but others will need to be managed. The way hedgerows are trimmed, and when and how often this is done, has a huge influence on wildlife. The more that we can do to increase a hedgerow's natural value, the better, while bearing in mind practicality and costs for owners and managers.

The following are the most important aspects for hedgerow management that relate to wildlife.

Field margins, often not cut by the silage harvester have a more diverse flora where fertiliser and slurry are excluded. (Photo: Catherine Keena).

SHAPE AND SIZE

In general, a hedge which is wide at the base, relatively tall (3 metres plus) and dense, with some mature trees, with an uncultivated, wide margin and a drain, is ideal for wildlife. In other words, the more it becomes like a strip of woodland, the better.

In general, the taller and fuller the hedge, the more bird species are associated with it. There are some exceptions: Yellowhammers, which like tillage land, prefer shorter, trimmed hedgerows.

An investigation of habitat selection in hedgerow nesting birds in med-west Ireland found that the largest hedgerows have the greatest habitat diversity and thus will support the greatest number of bird species. Hedgerows with well developed herb, shrub and tree layers are the most valuable and clearly have the potential to support a range of bird species. Up to 14 bird species were recorded as holding territory in some of the best hedgerows, whereas in others only one species was recorded (Lysaght, 1990).

If the hedgerow is trimmed annually and kept short (e.g. less than 2 metres) and narrow (e.g. 1.5 metres wide or less), this will reduce the amount of nesting space and cover for birds, and there will be no fruit and berries — vital food for wild birds and mammals in winter.

Whitethorn trees allowed to mature within hedgerows. (Photo: Catherine Keena)

MARGIN

When the margin is narrow or non-existent, for example, when livestock graze down the base of the hedgerow consistently, this restricts the growth and variety of herbaceous plants and the invertebrates which live and feed on them. It also reduces the amount of cover for certain birds and mammals. Spraying herbicide along the grassy margins will have a similar effect. Margins which are fertilised or mown regularly will tend to have a different mix of wild flora to those which are unmanaged. Barn Owls can sometimes be seen hunting for small mammals along hedgerow margins, but only find their prey where the margins provide plenty of food and cover.

DENSE BASE

Dense growth at the bottom of hedgerows provides cover for birds, invertebrates and small mammals. Some examples include Wren, Dunnock, Hedgehog and Pygmy Shrew.

'ESCAPED' HEDGEROWS

Some hedges have 'escaped' to become a line of trees and have long ago lost their stockproofing function. Often, these 'neglected hedgerows' have no cover at the base, which also tends to be quite narrow. Again, this restricts the opportunities for birds which like to nest in dense cover. However, the trees themselves will allow dependent wildlife to survive there, and will provide food for birds in winter.

'RELICT' HEDGEROWS

Some hedgerows are thin and gappy, and are in the final stage of their life-cycle. Shrubs have died out and have not been replaced, hence the gaps. These 'relict' hedgerows are very important wildlife refuges. They are best left alone and preferably fenced to exclude livestock.

The Hedgehog and the Badger are two common nocturnal mammals associated with hedgerows. Hedgehogs eat slugs, worms and beetles. They hibernate over the winter in nests made of leaves. Badgers like to make their setts in woodland and sometimes in undisturbed hedge banks. Badgers eat earthworms, fruit, carrion, mice and young rabbits, all of which are to be found along a healthy hedgerow.

Hedgehog (Photo: Mike Brown)

Badger (Photo: Mike Brown)

32

Many species of birds roost, nest and feed in and around hedgerows. Long-tailed Tits (opposite) are commonly seen in small flocks which move through hedgerows and woods, hunting for insects. The Yellowhammer appears to be declining rapidly in Ireland due mainly to loss of arable land. The Linnet nests in dense, thorny hedgerows. It too has suffered a decline. Farmers in the REPS can opt to grow plots of crops to help Linnets and other seed-eating birds. The Song Thrush relies on hedgerow berries and fruits for food in the autumn. The tiny Wren likes dense hedgerows for nesting and feeds on insects and spiders found in the leafy cover.

Long tailed tits (Photo: Richard Mills)

Yellowhammer (Photo: Irish Birding Services)

Song thrush (Photo: Richard Mills)

Linnet (Photo: Irish Birding Services)

Wren (Photo: Richard Mills)

barn owl (Photo: Richard Mills)

Bank vole (Photo: Mike Brown)

Wood mouse (Photo: Mike Brown)

The Barn Owl is on the Red List of Birds of Conservation Concern in Ireland. Although Barn Owls prefer undisturbed old buildings for nesting and roosting, they sometimes nest in hollow trees. Hedgerow margins and other areas of rough ground hold the prey that the owls feed on. The native Field Mouse and the introduced Bank Vole are two such prey species which can be found along the hedgerow base, feeding on seeds, fruit and insects.

Hedgerows teem with invertebrates. Some of the most beautiful are the butterflies and moths. The caterpillars of Small Tortoiseshell and Peacock butterflies feed on nettles, often found growing in hedgerow margins. The food plant of the Brimstone butterfly is buckthorn. The Elephant Hawk Moth, so named because of the caterpillar's trunk-like 'snout', is found in hedgerows and gardens.

Grasshopper (Photo: Mike Brown)

Elephant hawk moth (Photo: Mike Brown)

Brimstone butterfly (Photo: Eddie Dunne)

Peacock butterfly (Photo: Mike Brown)

Small tortiseshell Butterfly (Photo: Mike Brown)

Hedgerows – vital connections for wildlife

We use roads and railways to connect with the world around us. Wildlife uses hedgerows and watercourses. Hedgerows provide refuges for woodland wildlife. If we had no hedgerows, wildlife would tend to be isolated in little 'islands' such as small woods and conifer plantations, surrounded by large areas devoted to agriculture. Intensively farmed land does not offer many opportunities for wildlife. Most plants and animals need "corridors" and "stepping stones" in order to maintain their populations and colonise new areas. Hedgerows allow animals which need cover, such as the Wood Mouse and the introduced Bank Vole, to travel. Other Irish mammals which regularly use hedgerows as corridors or to live are the Fox, Badger, Stoat, Hedgehog, Rabbit, Irish Hare, and Pipistrelle Bat.

The wildlife value of a hedgerow is enriched if it is near or connected to a woodland or other high-value habitat. Animals and plants tend to colonise such hedgerows more readily. Hedgerows and narrow strips of woodland alongside canals, rivers or wetlands can be rich in wildlife.

If we want to conserve this rich variety of creatures, we have to maintain the links with all these habitats, which would otherwise be fragmented. Hedgerows provide these links.

What types of hedgerows are most valuable?

In general, the more woody species there are in a hedgerow, the more associated species of animals and plants can occur. A hedgerow with only whitethorn will not attract as many associated species as one with whitethorn, blackthorn, bramble, elder, hazel, etc. Often, older hedgerows will tend to have more tree and shrub species, because it takes time for some species to colonise. For example, bramble is quick to colonise but hazel and holly can be much slower.

In Britain, a species-rich hedgerow is defined as one containing five or more native woody species on average in a 30 metre length. If the number of woody species is less than five, but the hedgerow has a rich herbaceous flora that includes primrose, wood anemone, bluebell, herb-robert and common dog violet, it is also deemed to be species-rich. In Northern Ireland, a species-rich hedgerow is defined as having six native woody species in a 30 metre

Hedgerows provide links with other habitats, in this instance a wetland. Hedgerows which are linked to high value habitats are especially worthy of conservation. (Photo: David Hickie)

length. On this basis, it is estimated that 37% (44,000 km) of hedgerows in Northern Ireland are species-rich. A survey of 120 hedgerows in Laois, Offaly and Wexford found similar levels of species-richness. The number of native woody species in a 30 metre stretch varied between 2 and 13 species, with approximately 35% of the surveyed hedgerows containing 6 or more native woody species. A total of *33* woody and climbing species were found (Feehan, 2002). A study of 516 hedgerows in the Castlerea district of North Roscommon found 31 woody species with an average of 4.59 per hedgerow. Whitethorn and bramble dominate with ash being far the most common hedgerow tree. Here, 30% of hedgerows contained 6 or more woody species (Kenny, 2004). Could one third of the island's hedgerows be species-rich and therefore worthy of special conservation measures? We will have to wait until the results of future surveys are made available.

HEDGEROWS: WATER AND WIND

Hedgerows bestow other benefits on us which we sometimes take for granted. We live in a wet and windy country and we are perhaps less aware of the important role that hedgerows play in moderating the effects of the weather.

HEDGEROWS REGULATE WATER FLOW

When parts of Brittany were seriously flooded in the early 1970s, the areas which had widespread hedgerow removal suffered the most. After this disaster, the French government introduced a scheme to encourage farmers to plant new hedgerows on the basis that they would pay for themselves as windbreaks, preventing soil erosion and providing a source of firewood. This is just one of many examples of how hedgerows and farmland trees can ameliorate the effects of adverse weather.

On sloping farmland, hedgerows and their drains intercept water running down the slopes and direct it towards streams, thus reducing soil erosion. Water can percolate more easily around trees and hedges, which reduces run-off.

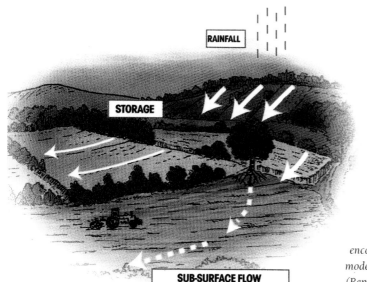

Hedgerows tend to slow water circulation and encourage percolation of water into the soil, thereby moderating the influence of floods and droughts. (Reproduced by kind permission of Solagro)

37

HEDGEROWS CAN IMPROVE WATER QUALITY AND REDUCE EROSION

Hedgerow networks generally slow the run-off of water and nutrients from the land. Hedgerows and their margins can act as a 'buffer strip', absorbing excess nutrients. Hedgerows and bankside vegetation protect river banks from erosion and subsequent siltation of rivers.

HEDGEROWS AS WINDBREAKS

The wind-sculpted whitethorns of the west of Ireland remind us that Ireland is indeed a windy island on the edge of Europe. Hedgerows make good wind breaks, because they filter the wind rather than block it. They provide shelter for up to thirty times their height. A dense base is more effective. Shelter offered by hedgerows can allow crops to germinate earlier because of higher soil and air temperatures (1-2 degrees Celcius and 4-5 degrees Celcius respectively), resulting in yields which can be higher. On the domestic front, houses surrounded by trees or hedgerows are more sheltered and will tend, therefore, to have lower heating bills.

The combined shelter effect of hedgerows in the landscape reduces the force of the wind at ground level. If all the hedgerows in an area were removed, the landscape would definitely feel windier and bleaker. So, not only do they act as windbreaks at the farm or house level but also contribute on a larger scale to the quality of life.

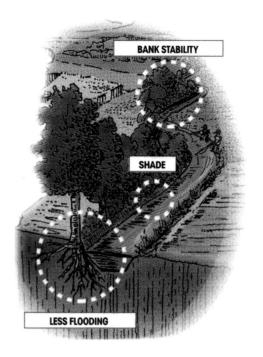

Trees and hedgerows along river banks filter pollutants from farmland and protect river banks from erosion. (Reproduced by kind permission of Solagro)

PRIVACY FROM PRYING EYES

As well as providing shelter from the wind and rain, hedgerows and their trees are very effective screens for houses and other developments. A well-treed landscape can visually accommodate more buildings than a bare landscape.

WOOD FOR FARM AND HEARTH

Hedgerow trees can be a source of high quality timber, depending on how they are managed. Timber is a carbon-neutral, renewable building material and, as firewood, a source of heat and electricity that can be grown in rural areas. Hedgerow trees may well be our most important resource of native Irish timber.

A native hedgerow in a public park bordering a housing estate in Dublin city. (Photo: David Hickie)

Hedgerows in the suburbs

Since hedgerows are traditional rural features, we tend to forget that they are also found outside farms. The housing boom has pushed the town into the country, and neighbouring farmland is gradually being covered by the incoming tide of concrete and tarmac. Occasionally, hedgerows manage to survive the bulldozers, where they become even more important for the maintenance of wildlife. Native hedgerows are some of the 'stepping stones' and corridors that wildlife needs if it is to thrive in the artificial world of towns and villages. Some wild species have adapted rather well to towns (such as the Magpie, the Fox and various garden birds) but other species need plants and habitats that are not usually found in urban settings.

GARDEN HEDGES

Garden hedges are very different from native hedgerows. They are usually composed of one species, such as ornamental privet (*Ligustrum ovalifolium*), holly, laurel, beech, *Forsythia* or

Townland boundary and other ancient hedgerows

Townlands are the smallest and most ancient divisions of the country and are often marked by large stone and earth banks which have developed into hedgerows over the centuries. John Feehan, in his book Farming in Ireland, describes these old hedge banks as being dominated by ash and hazel, their age and size making for a greater variety of niches, and so they are vitally important refuges for flora and fauna. "They are also monuments to the hands that laid out the land, as worthy of consideration as ringforts and burial mounds."

Unfortunately, very little survey work has been carried out on the natural history of these old hedgerows. This is obviously important, because they cannot begin to be protected if we don't know which ones are especially worthy of conservation. Ironically, some results of surveys can be found in Environmental Impact Assessments of road schemes, carried out by the National Roads Authority (see also Chapters 6 and 10). It is encouraging to note that some local authorities are planning to undertake hedgerow surveys (see Chapters 6 and 10).

Other old hedgerows include those which have developed or were originally planted around raths for defensive purposes, and these will have a very high heritage value. In these situations, management may have to be a compromise so that the archaeological or historical interest is preserved. However, in most cases, they will need simply to be left alone.

hornbeam, to name a few common examples. Often, the species planted are cultivated varieties of the wild species, planted for colour and interest, as well for as screening and privacy.

Hedgerows of Leyland cypress, often criticised, have proved extremely popular in Ireland, because they grow quickly and give 'instant shelter' and screening. In contrast, Lawson cypress, a more benign coniferous species was commonly planted around farmsteads.

Box (*Buxus sempervirens*) was commonly used for ornamental hedges in gardens, especially those of big houses. The tallest box hedge in the world can be found in Birr Castle demesne, Co. Offaly. The boxleaf honeysuckle (*Lonicera nitida*), so-called because its leaves resemble box, is a member of the honeysuckle family but is nothing like its fragrant climbing cousin, honeysuckle or woodbine (*Lonicera pericylmenum*). A common sight in many 1940s housing estates and public parks around the country, it was sometimes known as "poor man's box", because it grew faster and was cheaper to buy, and was not as neat or formal.

Garden hedges are often trimmed at least once every year and often much more frequently. Thus, neither flowers nor fruit are produced, and they lack the structural diversity of a good farm hedgerow, so the opportunities for wildlife are restricted. This does not mean that such hedges are worthless.

Garden birds such as Song Thrush, Blackbird, Wren and Robin will often nest in garden

hedges, or any shrubby growth that provides cover, even if these lack the variety of niches of their country cousins.

BLENDING 'NATIVE' WITH 'EXOTIC'
Native hedgerows can sometimes be found on housing estates and around one-off rural houses. Developers have tended to replace such native features with ornamental plantings, believing that it will make the development stand out against the more mundane adjoining countryside, and make management more convenient. It is possible to marry the native with the exotic. The retention of existing native hedgerows should be encouraged. Native trees and shrubs such as whitethorn, crab apple and wild cherry can complement exotic trees and shrubs which give colour in the autumn, such as maples and dogwoods. Native seed or cuttings, ideally taken from wild shrubs nearby, should be used, rather than imported stock.

Honeysuckle, or woodbine, emits its beautiful scent at dusk to attrace moths for pollination purposes. (Photo: Catherine Keena)

Poppies on a roadside verge.
(Photo: Gladys Hickie)

CHAPTER 4. HEDGEROWS IN THE LANDSCAPE

(Text and all images for Chapter 4 by Art **Art McCormack**)

The way we perceive the landscape depends on many different things. We have often heard the phrase: "Beauty is in the eye of the beholder". But perhaps there are some elements of our perception of the landscape that many of us share in common. The philosophy of aesthetics deals with the definition of beauty, attempting to understand that which inspires and moves us. The word aesthetics is understood here to involve perception in a broad sense, comprising that which appeals through the senses and is imbued with meaning of various kinds. This chapter uses aesthetics to explore how we see hedgerows in the landscape, and what this means to us.

Hedgerows: made by man but using nature's raw material

Hedgerows are an integral part of Ireland's lowland agricultural landscapes. Hedgerows and fields are complementary — one defines the other.

Hedgerows cover vast areas of the Irish countryside, but their size, shape and colour vary, depending on, for instance, soil, elevation, their style of management, their age, the county or region and the design of the hedge makers. Such variation contributes to distinction of landscape character and aesthetic quality. (See page 79).

All our landscapes, including hedgerows and fields, have been shaped by the human hand, with nature providing the 'raw material'. And so they embody a creative tension between nature and nurture, ecology and culture. This tension is at the heart of our aesthetic experience of hedgerows.

The cultural value of hedgerows reflects a variety of functions that they have fulfilled over the ages — farming, defence of ancient settlements, marking out of boundaries, providing food and shelter, and their place in the landscape, which helps us to define the rural space, all of which affect our aesthetic appreciation of hedgerows.

Hedgerows can be used to define space and control movement. This view depicts a carefully manicured avenue with a regular line of maples running alongside a clipped beech hedge, forming an avenue to a grand house.

There can be an ugly side to hedgerows – they are sometimes used for dumping!

Visual appeal of hedgerow flora – wild rose and elderberry.

Splendour of gorse hedgerows appeal not only to the eye, but also because of their rich fragrance and the sound of pods cracking in the sunshine

Whitethorn hedgerows, like snow drifts

Bottom left: The foliage of hedgerow trees can also provide visual appeal due to the contrast between summer and autumn colour.

Bottom right: This Fuchsia hedgerow provides a strikingly colourful delineation of roadsides and field boundaries.

We appreciate hedgerows with our senses as well as our mind and spirit, for it is not only *what* we see that matters but *how* we see. While it is through the eyes, ears, nose and hands that we sensually perceive, our minds give meaning. And through the spirit this meaning can sometimes touch an inner depth.

Hedgerows appeal to us visually

The most obvious aesthetic experience is the visual appeal of hedgerows — their pattern and profile in silhouette at a broad landscape scale and their shape, colour, texture and fragrance at a more intimate scale. These features give character to a particular landscape and give an identity to a townland or county. Perhaps the most obvious way that hedgerows appeal to us visually derives from the shapes, colours and fragrances of their flora.

43

A mechanically pollarded hedgerow viewed in silhouette can be sculptural in character

The rhythmic spacing of mature broadleaf trees rising from a tightly trimmed hedgerow creates an ordered aesthetic of an architectural kind.

The hedgerows in this view define a rhythmic field pattern and interlock with the forest to create a balanced composition that includes the rocky peak.

Top: An unusual sculptural effect resulting in a 'split' hedgerow has been created on the boundary between two farms, both of which are in the REPS but on different management timeframes.

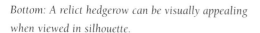

Bottom: A relict hedgerow can be visually appealing when viewed in silhouette.

While possibly poor in stock proofing, this hedgerow without undergrowth creates an elegant and finely formed sculptural effect which is almost Gothic in its architectural qualities.

Hedgerows help to create a sense of place

Hedgerows give character to a townland or a county, making it distinct from other areas. This gives us a *sense of place* which enriches our ' reading' of the landscape. We can also experience a sense of place where hedgerows enclose spaces, by particular or special hedgerows or where hedgerows are found together with other man-made features, such as lanes, feeding troughs or gateways.

Hedgerows appeal to us through a sense of utility and process

Hedgerows can be appreciated as part of a working landscape shaped by human hands over time. Order has been created on a previously natural landscape by means of disciplined and judicious management through the centuries. We can see this especially in an intensively farmed landscape where human mastery and control prevail and are expected.

Trimmed hedgerows with post and rail fencing in the stud farm area of Co. Kildare, engendering a clear landscape identity.

The avenue and hedgerows with large broadleaf trees combine to frame this Georgian house, creating a strong sense of place.

Young hedgerows along with their protective fencing communicate visually the processes involved as well as the function of the hedgerows as stock proof barriers.

Fuchsia hedgerows are common along the western seaboard, but are particularly associated with the Dingle Peninsula.

(Far right) A tree hut in a hedgerow expresses the building construction technique as well as its use for recreation

Intellectual appeal

The way we view hedgerows is enriched by an understanding of history, ecology, rural society or farming practices, all of which stimulate interest and deepen our aesthetic appreciation.

The remains of stone walls made with care, thought and skill inform the viewer of the mason's craft and regional tradition.

This combination of hedgerow, lane and troughs affect us intellectually and emotionally, stimulating a curiosity and nostalgia as well as possibly conjuring up memories of and associations with mythology and fairytales.

This pragmatic solution to providing water for cattle uses a riparian hedgerow as well as barbed wire for protection of the river bank against erosion while keeping separate the drinking pool.

The nature of hedgerows

Since nature in landscapes resonates deep within us, the natural elements in hedgerows appeal to us aesthetically. Just because a landscape is farmed, it does not mean that nature is absent, even where farming is intensive. The sense of nature and of a more natural landscapes can be increased by the relationship of hedgerows to their surrounds.

Wild flowers in the hedgerow leave room for Nature to take her own course.

Relict hedgerows, especially where overgrown by ivy, can be more natural looking than those that are neatly managed.

Even where fields are intensively managed, the herbaceous layer at the foot of the hedgerows, by being naturalistic, can enhance aesthetic experience.

The presence of water with hedgerows usually enhances the sense of nature and aesthetic appreciation.

Primal appeal of diversity

Hedgerows can appear to be of diverse structure, which people instinctively find attractive. This involves views that are (a) parkland-like across the landscape and (b) varied concerning light and shade along roads and lanes. Species diversity combined with variation in hedgerow structure result in contrast in light versus shade, openness versus enclosure and views versus containment.

A loosely structured parkland is particularly appealing, based on a primal instinctive recognition that such conditions provide good habitats for us as well as survival opportunities. Such varied structure and lighting also engender a sense of intrigue, stimulating a desire to penetrate into the landscape in order to experience and learn more.

The layering of mature broadleaf hedgerows as viewed obliquely can create the appearance of a parkland

This lime tree-formed grassy path creates both a rhythmic sequence and a partially obscured end which inspire one to walk and investigate.

(Above) A desire to enter and investigate is instilled by the view along this lane, where varied plant and spatial structure create dappled lighting and the end is partially obscured.

A similar sense of attraction and intrigue is instilled where adjacent hedgerows form a winding grassy path.

Spiritual association

This concerns a deep experience of the
mystery of life and death.

It could be prompted by autumn decay or
spring shoots. It can also occur when we are
within shadow looking towards light, for
example, where we are looking along a road or
lane that is enclosed, tunnel-like and darkened
by tall and overhanging hedgerows and where
brightness is visible beyond. A certain suspense
and anticipation may be created which can
consciously or subconsciously resonate with
the birth experience, or with what some
maintain is the journey through death, that is
the passage not simply from darkness to light,
but from one life to another. The intensity of
the experience is heightened where the road
steeply ascends towards the light. Regardless of
whether one has such a deep and personal
response, the experience of such conditions is
aesthetically potent and intense.

Hedgerows can be attractive when in leaf or
bare, tall or low, full or trimmed, continuous
or gappy. They can be homogeneous or varied,
or comprise native broadleaves or exotic
conifers and they still will hold appeal for us.
Relict hedgerows or those with overgrazed
stems may be undesirable for stock proofing,
but could be visually attractive as sculptural
features, especially when we see them in
silhouette against the sky or a lake.

There is a wonderful variety in Irish
hedgerows: their different shapes and sizes,
the way they were made, their composition of
trees and shrubs, their patterns in the
landscape and their range of meaning all play
a part in giving rural Ireland its local and
regional identity and enrich our aesthetic
experience.

*A powerful sense of compulsion is generated by the
contrasting darkness of this farm lane, created by tall
overhanging hedgerows, and the intense 'light at the
end of the tunnel' and accelerated towards this light
by the final climactic ascent of the lane.*

*The bursting forth of foliage or flowers, as in this
example of blackthorn, can instil an excitement about
birth and new life.*

Chapter 5. Managing farm hedgerows – a manual of best practice

Hedgerows were originally planted with the aim of being managed by hand. The sole reason for management in the old days was to keep hedgerows stockproof. In the 21st century, wire and electric fencing, often in addition to a hedgerow, can control the movement of livestock, so some farmers feel they do not have to manage their hedgerows. The practice of management was never embraced with as much enthusiasm here as in Britain. Arthur Young, our intrepid 18th century commentator, remarked that, even in the late 18th century, many hedgerows were "ragged, and open at the bottom, and full of gaps whole perches long."

Maintaining a hedgerow using the traditional manual methods is time-consuming, tough, physical work, and now nearly all managed hedgerows are trimmed mechanically. It is important to emphasise that much of rural Ireland was never 'manicured', and its charm and identity derives from the 'minimal maintenance' approach. If the pendulum was to swing the other way, hedgerows would be trimmed within an inch of their lives, which would be far more undesirable and damaging. Therefore, if some farmers choose not to cut their hedgerows, then that is their choice, and it should be respected. They are contributing in no small way to the beauty and character of their locality.

No single method of management is appropriate for all hedgerows. (Photo: Catherine Keena)

(Photo: Catherine Keena)

The guidelines in this book are designed for landowners whose hedgerows are already managed, or have 'escaped', i.e. where they have grown tall and leggy but have not yet become a line of trees. Relict hedgerows, which are very important for the landscape and wildlife, are best left alone. Hedgerows differ in size, shape, age, how they have been managed in the past, their proximity to other habitats, in their content of shrubs and trees, whether or not they are on farms, the type of farm (e.g. livestock, tillage, market garden), whether they are along roadsides, in parks or in suburban areas. These considerations have to be borne in mind when considering how to manage them. Practicality and cost are also important.

The best practice techniques that we have set out below are aimed at fulfilling a number of important objectives. These include:

- Stock control and shelter
- Maintenance of biodiversity – conservation of wild plants and animals
- Maintenance and enhancement of the rural landscape
- Maintenance of our rural heritage — culture, history and archaeology

Types of hedgerows

For the purpose of management, hedgerows can be classified into a number of different types:

Hedgerows with a dense base – hedgerows which are trimmed periodically, sometimes as frequently as once a year and are generally stockproof.

'Escaped' hedgerows – hedgerows which, through lack of management, have grown too high and 'escaped', losing their dense base but have not yet become a line of mature trees with a full canopy. These hedgerows are typically thin at the base, with perhaps some gaps, and are no longer stockproof.

Relict hedgerows – hedgerows where the shrubs have grown into mature trees with a full canopy, while others have died out and have not been replaced, leaving large gaps.

Hedgerow with a dense base trimmed to a triangular shape, leaving saplings. (Photo: Catherine Keena)

Escaped hedgerow. (Photo: Catherine Keena)

Relict hedgerow. (Photo: Catherine Keena)

(Right and below): Trimming a hedgerow sloping the sides from a wide base, avoiding the 'flat' top, with circular saw and flail. (Photos: Bomford and Catherine Keena)

(Below): Trees which are allowed to grow tall provide song posts and food for birds and enhance the beauty of the hedgerow. (Photo: Catherine Keena)

Management guidelines for farm hedgerows

HEDGEROWS WITH A DENSE BASE

Healthy dense growth at the base of the hedgerow keeps it stockproof. Routine trimming is required to retain a dense base and prevent hedgerow woody species growing into mature trees.

How often should one trim? – While light annual trimming can benefit the hedgerow, it is not good for wildlife, as flowers or fruit are not produced. The best compromise is usually to trim every three years in rotation around the farm. This will leave some areas undisturbed for wildlife. While growth rate varies, three-year growth can usually be trimmed satisfactorily with the flail machine.

What is the best shape? – Side-trimming to a triangular shape is recommended, leaving the peak as high as possible, sloping sides from a wide base. This allows light to reach the base, encouraging dense growth. Currently, many hedgerows which are trimmed regularly need to be allowed to grow taller and wider.

Machinery — Clean cuts are essential. If a flail is used on stems over 12mm (or as thick as a man's finger) or if there is a poor edge on the flail the result is shattered and frayed branches. This can lead to disease and decay of the branches and ultimately damage to the fabric of the hedgerow. Use a circular saw on heavier growth when re-shaping thus avoiding frayed stems. Sharpen equipment as necessary.

Where to cut — Cut stems a little above the level of the previous cut, leaving up to 12 mm of current growth (see diagram). Cutting back to the same level depletes the energy of the shrubs, promoting a small number of long shoots rather than dense, vigorous growth.

When to trim? — Trim only from the 1st of September to the last day of February to avoid disturbing nesting birds. Trimming in late winter allows full use of the hedgerow's food resources.

Trees – Allow trees to develop at regular intervals along the hedgerow line. You will notice that fruit-laden branches are found on older growth. Such growth occurs in mature relict hedgerows. Leave the occasional tree, such as whitethorn, grow to maturity within routinely trimmed hedgerows. Suitable saplings should be identified and allowed to develop naturally. These are the young recruits which will, in time, grow to their full glory and replace the old. Old hedgerow trees – even those beyond their prime, should be retained.

Trees such as ash and sycamore, which have been routinely topped, grow as multi-stems, have timber of low value and weaken the fabric of the hedgerow. Select a leader by removing all but one stem. Remove unwanted saplings.

Quality sawn timber comes from straight, single-stemmed trees. This is achieved with regular formative shaping and high pruning. Trees should be protected from livestock . Attaching wire to trees reduces the financial value greatly as well as being dangerous when the tree is felled. Be careful when working

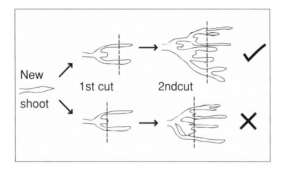

(Above): Elm identified and retained. (Photo: Catherine Keena)

(Left): Cut stems a little above the previous cut, resulting in dense vigorous growth.

machinery near the base of trees as roots can be inadvertently damaged. Always be aware of overhead wires.

'ESCAPED' HEDGEROWS

'Escaped' hedgerows have grown into tall stemmy plants, but not yet into mature trees. Trees have a natural lifespan, and given time and space, they grow, mature and die. Their lifespan can be extended by rejuvenation. Laying or coppicing can rejuvenate 'escaped' hedgerows. This involves major surgery. It should only be carried out on healthy hedgerows, growing vigorously. If in doubt, try a short section to assess the response. If regrowth is slow, then it is best to leave alone.

Cutting thick stems too high produces growth at that height and not lower down, where it is needed to make a stockproof hedgerow.. (Photo: Catherine Keena).

Radical surgery for an escaped hedgerow. Stems are cut very close to the ground with a tractor-mounted circular saw. New shoots will emerge from the base, which will provide bushy growth where it is needed (Photo: Catherine Keena).

Pollarding or topping an escaped hedgerow produces bushy growth at the height of cut, and can encourage a gappy base. It is not generally recommended.

Method 1. Coppicing

Coppicing is an ancient technique for managing broadleaf woodland which has been brought into the modern age with the use of equipment that is quick and efficient. Hedgerow shrubs are cut as close to the ground as possible (about 100mm) with a chainsaw or tractor-mounted circular saw. A sloping cut allows rain run-off.

Frayed branches, resulting from the use of a flail, on stems which are too thick. (Photo: Catherine Keena).

- Coppicing should be carried out in winter, preferably before bud burst.
- After cutting and disposing of the brash, livestock must be excluded.
- Consider livestock reach and future access for machine trimming when positioning the fence. Temporary fencing allows flexibility for the future.
- Control competing vegetation as necessary.

Wire and nails secured to trees can damage saws and can be dangerous for hedge cutting operators. (Photo: Catherine Keena).

Summary guidelines for hedgerow trimming to benefit wildlife

These guidelines are not a prescription for all farmers. Some farmers choose not to trim their hedgerows.

• Trim hedgerows in rotation around the farm, so that some will always be left uncut.

• Aim to trim each length of hedgerow approximately every three years.

• Aim for a triangular 'A' shape and allow the top of the hedgerow to be as high as is practical.

• Aim to trim in late winter (January/February) if possible (but no later), so that vital berries, fruits and nuts remain available as food for wildlife throughout the autumn and early winter.

• Try to avoid spray drift and fertiliser from reaching/affecting the hedgerow. If possible, leave a field margin at least 1.5 metres between the pasture or crop and the hedgerow base.

• Leave some trees, including thorns, to grow to their full height at intervals.

The ideal hedgerow shape for wildlife is tall, wide and dense at the base, with a wide, uncultivated, grassy margin.

This hedgerow is wide, fairly tall and dense, with generous margins, all of which are good for wildlife. (Photo: David Hickie).

• New growth can be trimmed as necessary, gradually shaping to a triangular shape.
• Infill gaps with quicks into suitably prepared ground – dig in well-rotted farmyard manure.

For more information on planting, see Chapter 7.

Method 2. Laying

Laying is another old technique for reinstating a stockproof hedgerow. Coincidentally, it also happens to be a wildlife-friendly way. Unlike coppicing, the hedgerow stems are not removed, but are cut three-quarters of the way through, near the base, with a sharp blade and bent over at an angle. New shoots grow from below the cut stump at ground level, thickening the hedgerow base. The rejuvenated hedgerow can be left to grow or 15-20 years and laid once more as it becomes gappy. Alternatively, it can be routinely trimmed as a hedgerow with a dense base.

Laying Hedgerows

Hedge laying is a traditional skill which is now supported under the Rural Environment Protection Scheme.

Hedge-laying was rare in Ireland. It is more associated with Britain where it is a long-established skill. It is tough work but rewards the dedicated owner with a hedgerow that will remain dense and stockproof for far longer than a hedgerow which is managed mechanically.

(Right):
Laying hedgerows:
1. Trimming the sides
2. First cut
3. Second cut
4. Laying over
5. Cleaning the stump

RELICT HEDGEROWS
Relict hedgerows have become a line of mature trees and shrubs. The trees have a distinct bole and full canopy, and gaps are common. In this situation, it is too risky to rejuvenate. They can be treated as strips of old woodland, of great value for wildlife and the landscape.

These hedgerows should not be 'topped' but side trimmed if necessary. Fencing off from both sides prevents deterioration by stock tramping through the gaps and allows scrub to develop.

Chapter 6. Hedgerows, roads and houses

Most of us view the countryside from the road, whether we are walking along a boreen on a summer's evening or driving along a main road on the way to work. Therefore, roadside hedgerows tend to make more of an immediate impression on us than the internal hedges of farms. Where roadside hedgerows are trimmed short, we are allowed to see into the landscape beyond. Where they remain tall and overhang the road, we feel like we are travelling through a tunnel, eagerly anticipating the next glimpse of the landscape when we emerge at the other end.

"Roadside hedgerows have to be managed for road safety and access"

Roadside hedgerows differ from other hedgerows in one essential respect: they cannot be left to grow unhindered. They must be managed for road safety and vehicular access. Local authorities are legally responsible for ensuring that traffic can pass along national, regional, local and minor roads. The National Roads Authority (NRA) is responsible for the design and building of national roads, but not their maintenance. Roadside hedgerows are also managed by

A well-maintained roadside hedgerow shaped in an 'A' shape with a young oak allowed to grow through it. (Photo: David Hickie)

Roadside verges are often mown once a year and not treated with herbicides, both of which help wild flowers to flourish. (Photo: David Hickie)

utility companies, principally the ESB and Eircom, which have to maintain their networks. Trees and hedgerows have to be cut back where they obstruct or otherwise interfere with cables and pylons.

Hedgerows blocking progress?

If hedgerows were not trimmed periodically, they would grow across the road, eventually blocking our progress! This is indeed what appears to be happening in some counties. For example, it was reported in the local press, in the summer of 2004, that Galway County Councillors were receiving complaints from constituents that overgrown hedges and roadside verges were creating traffic hazards around the county. Galway County Council

was considering cutting roadside verges twice a year where they were obstructing motorists. In the same year, it was reported that Waterford County Council was to seek clarification from the Department of Environment if landowners could cut overgrown hedgerows on narrow county roads during the summer months for road safety reasons.

"Local authorities have to consider the needs of road users and wildlife"

The reason for this controversy? Local authorities are not only required to maintain roadside hedgerows for road safety and vehicular access but also must take into account the needs of wildlife. This dual responsibility is not new. The 1925 Local

59

(Above) Trimming in summer kills nesting birds. (Photo: David Hickie)

(Left) Thrush's nest (Photo: Catherine Keena)

Government Act required landowners to keep roads free from obstruction. If they didn't, the local authority could get a court order to force them to do this, or in extreme cases, they could carry out the work themselves and recover the costs from the landowner. But the Act expressly forbade hedgerow trimming from the end of March to the end of September each year. Now, the Roads Act, 1993 defines the legal responsibility of local authorities for the public road network, and landowners are served with notices to cut hedgerows, as with the 1925 Act.

Currently, the Wildlife Acts control the seasonal timing of hedgerow trimming. It is now illegal to trim hedgerows between the 1st of March and the 31st of August each year.

Hedgerows may be trimmed during this 'closed season' for overriding health and safety reasons, and local authorities must prove their case to the National Parks and Wildlife Service (NPWS) if required. Even local authorities, which themselves issue orders to landowners

Roadside hedgerows must be trimmed low at junctions for visibility. (Photo: David Hickie)

to maintain roadside hedgerows, can be prosecuted if they fall foul of the law. For example, Galway and Leitrim county councils were prosecuted and fined in 2002 and 2003 respectively for trimming roadside hedgerows during the closed season.

The various laws covering hedgerows and their management are detailed in Chapter 10.

Rare / threatened hedgerow plants

The Irish Red Data Book of Vascular Plants is an inventory of rare and threatened plant species in Ireland. No such species are confined to hedgerows but nevertheless they provide a habitat for some of them. Rare and threatened species of any plant or animal are a priority for conservation since if no action is

taken, they could become extinct. Road and building development, along with agricultural improvement, threaten some of these plants.

Yellow archangel (*Lamiastrum galeobdolon*), a perennial herb with whorls of yellow flowers, has been recorded from five counties, but more recently only in Dublin, Carlow and Wicklow. It is found in hedgerows and woods. Some of its habitats have been destroyed in the past through building development and road widening. Betony (*Stachys officinalis*) is an erect perennial with whorls of reddish-purple flowers, found in open woods, hedgerows and grasslands.

Summary guidelines for trimming of roadside hedgerows

- Roadside hedgerows may have to be trimmed each year for road safety and vehicular access. However, the field side of hedgerows bordering the road may be left uncut for two or three years.

- Side-trim hedgerows, sloping from a wider base, aiming for a triangular shape.

- Hedgerow trees can be allowed to grow to their full height at intervals along a length of roadside hedgerow.

- 'Overgrown' hedgerows which are already tall and overhang the road can be side-trimmed.

- Hedgerows at junctions have to be trimmed for visibility for motorists. Where growth is vigorous, they may have to be trimmed twice a year, e.g. February and September.

Roadside verges can be mown in late February and/or in September. Particular mowing regimes of the grassy verge encourage the growth of wild flowers.

New roads:
do hedgerows have a chance?

All over Ireland, fast new ribbons of asphalt are replacing the winding, bumpy roads of a past age. The old roads cannot cope with the massive increase in traffic and more stringent road safety standards. The new routes slice through farms and gardens which have evolved over generations. If hedgerows, trees or any other features stand in the way, they are removed. Although the road building programme has wide public support, the sheer scale of the impact on rural Ireland has provoked protests among some local communities.

Replacing the irreplaceable?

Although trees and hedgerows are some of the primary victims of new roads, national road building projects often include imaginative re-planting and landscaping schemes. National road schemes are designed and funded by the National Roads Authority but the work is carried out by local authorities. Some local authorities aim to conserve hedgerows during construction of regional and local roads. For example, Leitrim County Council aims to protect hedgerows of particular ecological value in the county, which must first be identified by surveys.

New policies for protecting hedgerows

Many counties are now adopting heritage plans, and often these plans will include objectives to protect roadside hedgerows. For example, Leitrim County Council aims to establish demonstration sites of best practice for hedgerow management along road schemes. Many county councils support training for local authority staff on hedgerow management. Westmeath County Council, in partnership with Networks for Nature, aims to review its policy on removing hedgerows for new developments. Leitrim, South Tipperary, Kerry and Roscommon now support the annual Golden Mile competition, and other counties are aiming to follow their lead (see below, and Chapter 10).

The Golden Mile — by-ways rather than highways

Travelling along the small, winding roads and boreens of rural Ireland is a special pleasure. Despite the roaring Celtic Tiger, many have not been widened or re-aligned and have kept their character. Although traffic has increased, they are generally not over-run with trucks and tour buses and most of the traffic is local. Along these roads, the splendour and variety of Irish hedgerows is on full view. Many stretches of minor roads have their own unique character and features, comprising a combination of hedgerows, trees and wild flowers, banks and stone walls, gates and piers, wells and shrines, farmyards, gardens and houses. And every stretch of country road has its own stories.

According to John Devane, founder of the competition and a Tipperary farmer, 'The Golden Mile' is an initiative to encourage people living on rural roads to become more aware of the natural and built heritage along their roadsides, and where necessary, to protect and maintain it. The project was pioneered by the Tipperary LEADER Group and is supported by 25 partners from the community or voluntary sector, farming, and public and private sectors. The first 'Golden Mile' competition was held in 2000 as a Millennium project and has now become an annual event that is likely to continue into the future, subject to funding.

A section of rural road entered in the Golden Mile, Co. Tipperary. (Photo: John Devane)

The Field
by Liam O Comain

they have plotted it
for house erection
inevitably a part
of the mortgaged
property belt
where I have traversed
a verdure for seasons

collecting broken delph
and clay-pipe pieces
after the plough
had probed its womb
and during periods
of gestation leaving a form
upon a lushful surface
lying as if reflecting
or enclosing the sun's rays
in autumn while in winter
imprinting frosty stubble
hunting rabbits nibbling
a sparse coat
horses cows and sheep

have left their mark with
broken fences decaying dung
and wool streaked hedges
and man's need has added
to the condition with yields
of cabbages and potatoes
as well as rape and corn

and yet for some years
it has been fallow
no furrows criss-cross its
bumps where ferns sprout
alongside bent and vernal
grasses and bull rushes
embrace a once voluptuous breast

sharing a flank with double
macadamized tracks
and a slow encroachment
of semi-detached bungalows
soon it will be no more
this place where a field was loved

Reproduced by kind permission of Ireland's
Own

Groups of residents are encouraged to enter a mile stretch of county or minor road in the competition. In addition to the overall winner and first and second runner-up prizes, commendations are awarded to the 'best extension of a tidy town/village'; 'best new entrant'; 'best community effort'; 'traditional and manmade features'; 'best hedgerows'; and 'litter and rubbish free mile'.

The 'Golden Mile' concept can provide a very meaningful way for communities to improve their environment, and so add to the quality of life of local residents and add to the experience of tourists and visitors.
John Devane emphasises that the effort required for the 'Golden Mile' competition is different from that required for the Tidy Towns competition. He recognises that the character and beauty of Ireland's minor roads is best maintained by a minimalist approach. "The overriding guideline is, 'if in doubt, under-manicure'. Another useful guideline is, 'if it is not harming you or causing an obstruction, then leave it alone'!"

New houses in the countryside — is there room for hedgerows?

Ireland does not have the strong traditions of urban living of many of our European neighbours. The idea of urban living is seen by many as a foreign imposition, forced on us firstly by the Vikings, founders of Cork, Dublin, Limerick and Waterford, and then by the Normans.

Apart from Sweden and Finland, Ireland has the lowest population density of the EU15 and we have a strong cultural leaning to dispersed rural settlement, including one-off houses. Every time a new house, housing cluster or housing estate is built in a field, a length of hedgerow is lost, simply to gain access to the field. Many of these one-off houses are reached by narrow lanes, made for the horse and cart and farm animals. They cannot cope with oil delivery lorries, bin lorries and delivery vans, nor can locals pass each other in their cars when they meet head-on. For this reason, there has been an understandable tendency for such lanes to be identified for widening. When roads engineers are consulted by planning staff in relation to a planning application for a house down a narrow lane, their tendency has been to say something like, "could you please make it a condition of a grant of planning permission that they set back the site boundary by three metres from the existing roadside hedgerow/boundary? Then, when we come to widen the road, we won't have to knock the hedgerow/boundary ourselves and buy the three metre strip behind it from the owners. It'll already be cleared for us to lay tarmac on."

In recent years, more hedgerows are likely to have been lost due to road improvements and new building in fields than have been removed by farmers. This attitude is changing, partly because of growing awareness of the importance of hedgerows as part of our heritage and because even the 'Celtic Tiger' at its most ferocious couldn't possibly afford to widen every narrow lane in the land into a proper road.

Another reason why hedgerows are being lost on building sites is taste, or lack of thought or awareness. Some people positively want to live behind a painted, block wall, rather than a beautiful natural hedgerow, because that is what they have become used to expect as a house boundary in rural Ireland. Local authorities are increasingly encouraging people building one-off houses in fields to retain the existing boundary hedgerow, for its benefits to wildlife, aesthetics and shelter from the wind and rain. More sensible practices in relation to the siting, design and landscaping of one-off houses are also being promoted, to enable new houses to blend in with their surroundings and match the style of traditional houses.

Examples of positive policy in relation to hedgerows, taken from the South Tipperary County Development Plan, are given in the appendix.

If you want to help attitudes to hedgerows evolve, you should encourage your Local Authority to adopt similar progressive policies whenever it is producing its next County Development Plan. You may also wish to make

A minor road in Co. Tipperary.
(Photo: John Devane)

observations on planning applications for rural houses that would result in the loss of hedgerows and encourage your County's planners to make their retention a condition of any planning permission granted.

Finally, Local Authorities also act as housing authorities and, due to the size of their operations, are probably one of the major housing developers in many counties. Local Authorities should be encouraged to retain, manage and enhance existing hedgerows in new and proposed housing schemes.

The country comes to town: managing suburban hedgerows

The management of suburban hedgerows involves some of the same considerations as farm and roadside hedgerows. They will sometimes need to be trimmed periodically if they encroach on domestic dwellings or if they obstruct traffic or hinder access. However, they do not need to be made stockproof and can often be allowed to grow unhindered if they are not adjoining roads. Native hedgerows, where they occur, are likely to be survivors of the conversion from farmland, and offer nostalgic reminders of the former land use. They become especially valuable in ecological terms where they connect suburban areas with farmland, so maintaining networks which are so vital for wildlife. In some suburban areas, hedgerows have become reduced to sad repositories for refuse. Sometimes, native hedgerows can be found in parks managed by local authorities. More often, they have been removed during 'clean-ups' when they were considered 'untidy'. Although local authorities are more conscious of protecting roadside native hedgerows, those in public parks, gardens and local authority housing estates are still under threat from vandalism or removal and replacement with exotic species plantings. Periodic trimming in most cases may be all that is needed, but if they are remnant or relict hedgerows, they can be allowed to grow unchecked. They can also be fenced to give protection from trampling or vandalism.

Retaining native hedgerows should be considered as part of a move towards more naturalistic landscaping, which blends existing natural species and features with new designs.

Crab apple flowering in a roadside hedgerow. (Photo: Catherine Keena)

CHAPTER 7. PLANTING HEDGEROWS

New hedgerow linking wildlife habitats on the Teagasc farm in Athenry, Co. Galway. (Photo: Catherine Keena)

Planting a hedgerow is very similar to planting a grove of trees or a plantation. Shrubs and trees are planted in lines, specific distances apart, but the planting technique remains the same. The other main difference is that hedgerow shrubs are pruned and trimmed in a particular way, so that they form a line of bushes rather than a line of trees, as we shall see below.

Why plant new hedgerows?

The decision to plant a hedgerow could involve one or more of the following reasons:

- Shelter for livestock or crops
- Wildlife habitats on farms or roadsides, linking existing features
- A gardener may wish to create a shelterbelt to protect fruit and vegetables
- Screening for privacy or to disguise buildings, dwelling houses or farmyards
- Aesthetic reasons – blending new houses in rural areas into the countryside. This may be a condition of planning permission
- Safety – along carriageways, to create sightlines and landmarks for motorists
- Demarcation of boundaries – sites, roadways, fields, etc.

Planting a new hedgerow

Avoid planting hedgerows in areas where they do not traditionally grow, such as uplands, open wet grasslands, bogs and areas where dry stone walls are the visual boundary, Take care not to damage existing wildlife habitats.

Need will dictate location. Consider the prevailing wind and local climatic conditions.

Choice of species will depend on established objectives – a high proportion of thorny species are required for a stockproof hedgerow. A non-thorny species rich hedgerow may be more appropriate for an urban wildlife hedgerow.

CHOOSING SPECIES

- Native species, adapted to Irish conditions benefit wildlife more.
- Locally grown plants, tolerant of local conditions, are likely to thrive,
- Plants grown from locally collected seed conserves local provenance (origin), but this takes time, effort and patience
- Thorny species such as whitethorn or blackthorn are essential for a stockproof hedgerow.
- A variety of species provides a varied food supply throughout the year for more wildlife. Include another hedgerow species or climber approximately every metre. Include a nurse species such as alder.
- Include trees, singly or in groups, at irregular intervals, provided they will be allowed to grow up and are NOT topped when the hedgerow is routinely trimmed. Avoid trees that cast dense shade, such as sycamore, beech and chestnut.

For more information on growing trees from seed or cuttings and establishing a tree nursery, readers are referred to *Our Trees* (see Bibliography).

Whitethorn is recommended as the main hedging shrub on farms because it is thorny, more practical to manage as a hedge than other species and is good for wildlife. It is not as invasive as blackthorn, which suckers easily. Imported whitethorn saplings are often not as vigorous or as thorny as the native Irish stock.

Whitethorn can and should be mixed in with other woody species which also tolerate routine trimming:

- Blackthorn
- Holly
- Hazel
- Spindle
- Guelder rose

Consider climbers such as dog rose and honeysuckle. Others, such as bramble, will usually colonise of their own accord and do not need to be planted. A variety of species offer a varied food supply for wildlife and colour throughout the year.

Native trees can also be interspersed with the hedging shrubs, provided they are allowed to grow up and mature and are not topped when trimming the hedgerow. These include:

- Crab apple
- Wild cherry
- Oak
- Ash
- Alder, especially on wet sites

Trees such as beech, sycamore and horse chestnut, although found in old hedgerows, cast a dense shade, gradually shading out hedgerow shrubs beneath, causing gaps. Because of its shallow roots, ash is not recommended in tillage fields.

Where a hedgerow is not required to be stockproof, a varied mix of species offers a more wildlife friendly and visually appealing hedgerow. Consider willow hedgerows on wet sites and gorse on upland or exposed sites.

PLANTING

Weather: avoid waterlogged soil and very wet or frosty weather.

Timing: plant from late October to March. Autumn is best in free-draining ground, spring in heavy soil.

Site preparation: this is critical. Cultivation before planting is essential for optimum growth. Mounding is advisable on wet sites.

Fertiliser: dig in well rotted Farm Yard Manure to encourage growth.

Plants: two to three-year old plants are most suitable. Fibrous, healthy roots and thick lower stems are more important than height. Roots must be kept moist before and during planting to avoid drying out and dying.

Plant density and spacing: the function of the hedgerow will dictate density and spacing:

- for stockproof hedgerows use up to eight plants per metre. A staggered double row is

A selection of species of young hedgerow shrubs heeled in to prevent roots from drying out while planting. Kildalton College, Co. Kilkenny. (Photo: Catherine Keena)

Digging the trench (Photo: Catherine Keena)

Filling the trench with well-rotted manure to give the young shrubs a good start (Photo: Catherine Keena)

Hedging plants are dug in manually. In this example, a double row has been planted (Photo: Catherine Keena)

Young whitethorns are pruned to stimulate bushy growth, which will ultimately produce a stockproof hedgerow (Photo: Catherine Keena)

Plastic pulled over whitethorns with slits cut for other species. (Photo: Catherine Keena)

preferable with the plants in each row 250mm apart and with a gap of 300mm between rows.

- A single row at 300mm spacing between plants may be adequate, if well maintained and if all the plants survive.

Depth: plant at the same level as previously planted and firm in.

Pruning: whitethorn may be cut back to 75mm to promote basal growth. Because the stumps are covered with a layer of plastic to control weeds, pruning is done at planting.

MAINTENANCE
- Plant only the length of hedgerow you will maintain.
- Contol competing vegetation to prevent smothering and to allow lower branches develop, giving a dense base.
  - Manual weeding
  - Chemical herbicides: extreme care is needed as spray drift damages young hedgerow plants
  - Mulching immediatly after planting helps weed control. Mulches: wood chippings, paper or cardboard should extend 150mm outside the plants.
  - Place plastic over pruned whitethorns, cut slits around other species and retain with inert material such as gravel or field stones.
- Exclude livestock using temporary fencing. Consider livestock reach and future access for machine trimming when positioning the fence. Rabbit-proof fencing may be needed if these are a problem locally.
- Replace dead plants.

- For the first few years after planting, it may be beneficial to cut whitethorn back to 75mm above previous level of cut, gradually shaping into a triangular shape.

Bushy growth after pruning (Photo: Catherine Keena)

It is likely more hedgerows will be planted in the countryside over the next few years. New stockproof hedgerows are valuable additions to farms, wildlife and the countryside.

Whitethorns pruned at planting and again the following winter to get a dense base. (Photo: Catherine Keena)

Wouldn't it be nice to think our generation will leave a lasting positive impression on the landscape? Wouldn't it be nice to think we can do so on our own farms, in our gardens and in the locality? Hedgerows remain long after those who plant them. (*Maireann an crann, ach ní mhaireann an lámh a chur é*).

(Photo below: Catherine Keena)

CHAPTER 8. MANAGEMENT PLANS FOR HEDGEROWS

Willow or sally hedgerow (Photo: Catherine Keena)

Gorse or Furze hedgerow.
(Photo: Catherine Keena)

Plan for the future

Hedgerows vary with pronounced regional differences. Underlying factors such as geology, soil type and climate create variation. Farming systems also have an influence. No single method of management is appropriate for all. Method of management will depend on the objective i.e. do I wish to have a stockproof hedgerow. Evaluate each hedgerow before deciding on management. Consider the long-term effect of current management. What will the hedgerow look like in twenty years?

On a farm a management plan should be drawn up for all hedgerows. Decide on objectives for sections of hedgerows. Management may be planned for future years. Having a plan with objectives will prevent inappropriate management being carried out in the meantime. Plans can and should change in time depending on circumstances and experience gained.

Assess hedgerows

On site assessment of all hedgerows is required prior to drawing up a farm hedgerow management plan. Consider the following:

- Type of hedgerows
- Previous management history.
- Condition
- Age
- Species richness – whether composed of only one or two shrub species or of several
- Species rareness

- Presence and frequency of trees;
- Location – their location relative to other habitats
- Location within designated areas such as Natural Heritage Areas, Special Areas of Conservation or Special Protection Areas.
- Archaeological or historical value – Townland boundaries
- Contribution to visual value of the surrounding landscape
- Contribution to amenity value of the surrounding landscape
- Contribution to cultural value of the surrounding landscape
- Adjacent features
- Adjacent land use
- Responsiveness to specific management
- Objectives for the future function of the hedgerow.

Decide on management aims

The extent and state of repair of hedgerows on the farm must be established and used to draw up an appropriate conservation and maintenance programme. Actions required should be clearly outlined to maintain and conserve these farm habitats and features. These actions should be considered against the landscape character of the area and how they will contribute to the environmental and amenity value of the farm and surrounding countryside. Management may be limited by cost, practicality and personal preference and interest. Where the extent of planned hedgerow management is limited, priorities should be established. Those of greatest ecological value and those most prominent in the landscape should be selected for maintenance.

Where major wildlife habitats exist on farms consideration should be given to allowing hedgerows that adjoin and link these areas to grow naturally. In general increasing the variety of hedgerow types in terms of height, width, shape and species mix will promote diversity in flora and fauna. The most valuable species for wildlife include oak, birch, mountain ash, whitethorn, alder, willow, ash, holly, crab and scots pine.

Hedgerows were not initially established for their ecological value. They still play an important practical role in farming. Fences often replace hedgerows, but in the long term are as costly to maintain as stockproof hedgerows. The loss of some hedgerows can be compensated for to a considerable extent by devoting greater attention to maintaining the quality of those that remain.

This hedgerow which is valuable to wildlife also provides valuable shelter to livestock. (Photo: Catherine Keena)

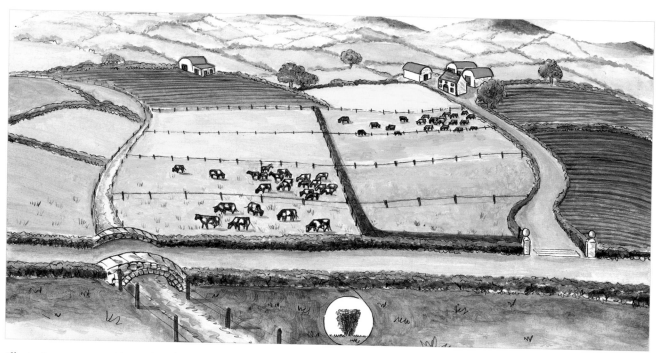

Illustration:
Monica
McCormick

Above: *Open bare landscape with few, very low treeless hedgerows*

Below: *Future possibilities for this landscape to improve wildlfe, shelter and scenic appearance, while continuing to farm intensively:*

- *Existing hedgerows maintained to a triangular shape, varying in height but allowed to grow as high as practical*
- *Occasional saplings of all species, including thorns, selected over time and allowed to grow to maturity, giving a range of ages of trees within the hedgerows*
- *Some hedgerows allowed to grow freely and escape*
- *New hedgerows planted along the existing permanent wire fences.*

Hedgerows give the Irish landscape its distinctive character and field pattern and provide an important wildlife habitat especially for woodland flora and fauna. Mature flowering hedgerows, predominately of whitethorn, provide a strong visual impact in the countryside during May and June each year. A balance of young and mature whitethorn is required for continuity. An appropriate conservation and maintenance programme promotes vigour, flowering, fruiting, and wildlife potential of hedgerows.

A variety is best. The quest for neatness should not take precedence over ecological and landscape considerations.

Mature hedgerows

Mature hedgerows should be allowed to grow freely and naturally. Maintenance in these situations should be confined to control of invasive species to prevent field encroachment. Where there are no mature hedgerows on a farm, selected sections should be allowed to develop and blossom freely.

In these instances maintenance should be confined to the light trimming of the sides to curtail outward spread. If necessary, remove overhanging lower branches interfering with normal machinery operations. Side trimming, where required, should be carried out on a two or three year cycle.

Over-managed hedgerows

Inappropriate or untimely maintenance often result in the weakening and ultimate demise of a hedgerow. Where they have been cut too often and too low, allow to grow unchecked to regain height and vigour. The extent of recovery will indicate what further action is required.

Trees

If it is decided to allow sapling trees to develop these should be selected singly or in groups at irregular intervals and allocated sufficient space to grow. Where mechanical trimming is required those saplings identified for retention should have the vegetation around them cleared manually and clearly marked to alert the machine operator.

Smooth wood species such as ash and sycamore when topped respond by throwing up many vertical shoots with little lateral growth. Hedgerows consisting a high proportion of these species, which have previously not been managed, should only be side trimmed where necessary. Remove unwanted saplings.

Escaped hedgerows

Hedgerows with little basal growth if left alone will grow into mature relict hedgerows. It may be more appropriate to rejuvenate the hedgerow by laying or coppicing distinct sections over the period of the plan. Careful consideration should be given when prescribing the lowering of the height of a hedgerow. Topping of hedgerows consisting of mature previously unmanaged whitethorn/blackthorn may also result in undesirable growth characteristics such as bushy top-heavy growth (the "toilet brush" effect).

A Tipperary farmer and his Teagasc adviser discuss a newly planted hedgerow. (Photo: Catherine Keena)

Ivy provides valuable cover for birds, bats and butterflies. (Photo: Catherine Keena)

Gappy hedgerows

Gaps may be closed by inplanting. Plant blackthorn quicks, or other suitable shade tolerant species such as holly in well prepared ground. Once established, whitethorn can be cut back 75 mm to promote growth. Keep weed free and protect from stock until established.

New hedgerows

Consider planting new hedgerows. The choice of site for a new hedgerow is important. Aim to shelter, augment or link existing habitats, such as woodland, scrub, ponds, watercourses or wild bird cover crops.

Ivy

Wherever possible, retain ivy and allow it to develop. Ivy is not a parasitic plant. Small rootlets of climbing shoots help ivy to adhere, but do not penetrate or feed on trees. Neither do they restrict trees as tree ties may do if left too tight. While trees are in good health, ivy does no harm. If trees decline for some reason such as Dutch Elm Disease, ivy takes over. However its sheer weight may make a tree more liable to wind blow. Where deemed necessary, ivy should be managed. It can be allowed to develop on some trees but controlled on others. It can also be allowed to grow unchecked for many years and controlled when growth becomes heavy.

Where ivy infestation is a risk to the stability or long-term viability of a hedgerow it should be controlled. If required to control ivy on trees, cut the stem just above ground level. Make a second cut ten centimetres above the first. Remove the section of stem.

Choose appropriate management

- Carry out hedgerow maintenance between September 1st and the last day of February to avoid the bird nesting season. Late winter is best, affording wildlife the opportunity to fully exploit the hedgerows food reserves.
- Before cutting, inspect the hedgerow to identify trees and other wildlife features, as well as obstacles or hazards.
- Some decisions such as changing the frequency of trimming are easy to implement.
- Retain old trees and standing dead trees
- There is considerable wildlife and landscape benefit if maintenance is carried out in rotation to ensure that there is growth at all stages both on the farm and in association with neighbouring farms.
- If possible, one side of a hedge should be trimmed in a season.
- Where hedgerows are cut, aim for a triangular shaped profile with a bushy

structure for maximum protection from wind. This will encourage the development of a dense hedge. A variety of heights is desirable.

- The crushing of hedgerows by heavy machinery is not permitted under REPS. While shrubs respond to any interference with a spurt of growth and appear to be ok, disturbance of roots caused by this method is harmful. Finger bar cutters utilising a pair of reciprocating blades are very suitable for trimming young growth. A flail cutter should only be used on soft growth of thorny species and beech, up to three years old. A flail cutter should never be used on heavy woody growth: resultant ragged ends invite disease and are unsightly. A circular saw may be used when coppicing or re-shaping is required.
- Fencing wire should not be attached to hedgerow trees and shrubs.
- Where practicable hedge trimmings should be piled in a non-intrusive manner to provide habitat. If hedge trimmings are to be removed this should be done as soon as possible after cutting.

Summary

- Draw up a plan
- Assess all hedgerows on the farm
- Decide on objectives for each – a variety in the countryside and on the farm is recommended
- Choose appropriate management
- Review results of management and adjust as necessary
- Consider planting new hedgerows

Choose appropriate management for three hedgerow types:

1. Hedgerow with a dense base.
2. Escaped hedgerow.
3. Relict hedgerow.

Hedgerow with a dense base trimmed in September, sloping the sides from a wide base and leaving mature trees and saplings, including thorns at irregular intervals. (Photo: Catherine Keena)

Escaped hedgerow which can be allowed grow into a relict hedgerow or rejuvenated by laying or coppicing. (Photo: Catherine Keena)

The wildlife value of these relict hedgerows is in the canopy, which provides food, shelter, home and highway for birds, bats and other species. Leave alone. (Photo: Catherine Keena)

Hedgerows Determining Alternative Landscapes

Hedgerows play a key role in the character of rural Ireland. We must accept in principle that landscape character will change with shifts in agricultural and other landuse policy. But we also need to anticipate trends and try to decide what sort of landscapes are desirable while providing the best balance regarding aesthetic, economic, environmental and social requirements.

Where the emphasis is on nature conservation, increase in hedgerow thickness including variety of structure and composition, even to the point of extensive encroachment on agricultural land, might be sought. If maximum agricultural yield and efficient use of farm machinery is required, then some hedgerow removal will likely occur. However, if traditional landscapes are preferred, then an effort must be made to keep farmers on the land maintaining the landscape.

(Photos: Art McCormack)

Drumlin with most hedgerows removed – a 'green egg' effect

Drumlin with traditional hedgerow and field pattern

Drumlin with encroached scrub freshly cut back

Drumlins with typical encroachment into fields

Drumlins with extensive encroachment, radically transforming landscape character

Chapter 9. Hedgerow contractor certification scheme

Have you ever wondered who trims hedgerows? Tom Murphy explains the part played by hedge cutting contractors.

The majority of hedgerows in Ireland are cut or trimmed by specialist contractors. However, landowners ultimately gives instructions on how they want their hedgerows dealt with.

The Wildlife Act, 1976, and the Wildlife (Amendment) Act, 2000, stipulate that, with certain exemptions, hedges may not be cut between 1st March and 31st August in order to protect wildlife during the breeding season. Local authorities can trim during this period if road safety is an issue (see also Chapter 6). However, it should be said that if landowners and local authorities had a hedgerow maintenance work programme in place, only minimal trimming should be required during the closed period.

Whilst we do not want to see an unmanaged countryside, neither do we want hedgerows manicured to within an inch of their lives by over-zealous use of mechanical hedgecutting equipment. At a PAC Ireland Hedgecutting Conference in 2003 contractors, recognising that hedgerows are a valuable habitat for wildlife, are an economic and environmentally friendly means of stock control and shelter and also help to reduce soil erosion and prevent the spread of disease, voted unanimously to support a Hedgecutting Training Course.

What is the PAC?

Professional Agricultural Contractors Ireland (PAC) is the representative association for agricultural contractors. PAC Ireland was founded in the 1970s and its members provide a vast range of mechanical services to farming, local councils and the amenity sector. Hedge cutting contractors are one of the many groups PAC Ireland represents. This sector also provides a hedge laying and maintenance service.

High on the list of PAC Ireland's priorities is that its members are properly insured, have a health and safety statement in place and provide a professional service. PAC Ireland's policy is to ensure that its members are up to date with European and national legislation and local authority bye-laws that affect their businesses and wherever possible, initiates training courses and educational seminars to facilitate this policy.

As a result, Networks for Nature and PAC Ireland entered into discussions with Teagasc to initiate a voluntary hedgecutting training course that would include the environmental impact of hedgerows, hedgecutting techniques

Hedgecutting contractors attending a Teagasc Hedgerow Management and Mechanical Hedgecutting course in Gurteen College, Co. Tipperary. (Photo: Catherine Keena)

required for different hedges, correct use and maintenance of machinery and health and safety issues. A programme was developed leading to FETAC qualifications. It includes a two-day course, leading to a certificate demonstrating proficiency in the use of mechanical hedgecutters. Teagasc delivers the programme in four colleges – Ballyhaise, Gurteen, Pallaskenry and Kildalton.

Hedgecutting contractors who have taken part in the course will now play a vital role in the maintenance and management of Irish hedgerows not only by using the correct cutting and trimming techniques but also by advising farmers and landowners on best practice in maintaining their hedgerows.

Tom Murphy is the Director of PAC Ireland and a member of the Steering Committee of Networks for Nature.

* FETAC: Further Education and Training Awards Council

CHAPTER 10. THE LAW, POLICIES AND INCENTIVES

Our new-found awareness of hedgerows has begun to be translated into laws and schemes whereby they can be protected and maintained. This chapter lists laws, policies and grant schemes which are relevant to hedgerows.

Legislation

The following section summarises the legislation relevant to hedgerows. Sources for this legislation are included in Appendix 2.

The Wildlife Act, 1976, as amended by the Wildlife (Amendment) Act, 2000

The Act gives some protection to wildlife in hedgerows. Under Section 40 of the 1976 Wildlife Act, as amended by Section 46 of the Wildlife Amendment Act, 2000, it is forbidden to cut or remove hedgerows or to destroy other vegetation during the bird nesting season, from the 1st of March to the 31st of August each year. It also stipulates that public works involving the distrubance of hedgerows during this period may only be carried out for reasons of public health and safety. There are some exemptions to these restrictions, mainly in the interests of agriculture.

The Act gives protection to areas designated by the Government as Natural Heritage Areas (NHAs). Hedgerows within such designated areas can therefore receive some protection.

A number of species of animals and plants are protected under the Wildlife Act. However,

there are exemptions for agriculture and public works. It is not an offence to interfere with a protected species unintentionally. Certain protected species can be found in association with hedgerows. For example, the Sparrowhawk and Barn Owl are two species which hunt alongside hedgerows, and may nest in hedgerow trees. Most of Ireland's wild birds and mammals are protected. Those which have an association with hedgerows include several bat species, Hedgehog, Red Squirrel, Stoat, Pine Marten, Irish Hare and Badger. The Fox, Rabbit, Wood Mouse, House Mouse, Bank Vole, Grey Squirrel, Brown Rat and Black Rat are not protected.

The Wildlife Act, 1976 also protects wild flora, by means of the Flora Protection Order, 1999 (S.I. No. 94 of 1999). Sixty-nine species of vascular plants and twenty-one species of lower plants are currently protected.

The Forestry Act, 1946

The Forestry Act prohibits the felling of any tree over ten years old unless the Forest Service has granted the landowner a felling licence. The exemptions include: trees held or managed by any Minister for Arts, Heritage Gaeltact and the Islands; trees in a borough or urban district; trees standing within 100 feet of any building other than a wall or temporary structure; trees cut down by local authorities in connection with public works or by public utilities such as the ESB or Bord Gáis; trees dangerous to road traffic; dead or dying trees and commercial fruit trees. The Forestry Act defines a tree as that which has a crown. Therefore, strictly speaking, some hedgerow trees come under this definition.

The Habitats Directive (Council Directive 92/43/EEC of 21 May 1992 on the conservation of natural habitats and of wild fauna and flora) – otherwise known as the 'Habitats Directive'.

The main thrust of the Habitats Directive is to protect important habitats or rare or endangered species throughout the European Union. However, one section is relevant to hedgerows. Article 10 requires Ireland and other EU countries to encourage, particularly in their planning and development policies, the management of features of the landscape which are of major importance for wild fauna and flora. Such features are those which, by virtue of their linear and continuous structure (such as rivers and riverbanks or hedgerows) or their function as stepping stones (such as ponds or small woods), are essential for the migration, dispersal and genetic exchange of wild species. The interpretation of this article is that local authorities have a legal responsibility to protect hedgerows where they are linked with designated European sites, i.e. Special Areas of Conservation (SACs) or Special Protection Areas for birds (SPAs), or where animal or plant species listed in the Directive may be found.

European Communities (Natural Habitats) Regulations, 1997 (S.I. No. 94 of 1997)
The regulations transpose the Habitats Directive into Irish law. Among other things,

they require planning authorities to assess the likely impacts that a development may have in or adjacent to a designated European site (i.e. an SAC or SPA). The law is only relevant to hedgerows if they are included in a designated site or where their removal might affect such a site.

Roads Act, 1993
Under the Roads Act, the breasting and topping of a roadside hedge is legally required in order to maintain a clear carriageway and vertical and horizontal sight-lines to ensure vehicular and pedestrian safety.

Under the Roads Act, 1993, as amended, a road authority (i.e. the National Roads Authority, Local Authorities) must prepare an Environmental Impact Statement (EIS) for motorways and for dual carriageways over 8 kms in a rural area and over 500 metres in an urban area. An EIS is a comprehensive study of the likely effects of a development on the environment.

An Bord Pleanála (the Planning Appeals Board) is the authority which assesses the EIS and has the legal powers to approve or refuse permission for a road scheme.

The Roads Act also provides for the preparation of an EIS for other road schemes where An Bord Pleanála considers that the construction of the proposed road would be likely to have significant effects on the environment.

The preparation of the EIS is carried out in parallel with the preliminary design of the scheme. As environmental impacts are identified, the necessary changes and/or ameliorative measures can be incorporated into the scheme design.

Planning and Development Act, 2000

Local authorities do not have direct powers to protect hedgerows, although they do have powers to manage roadside hedgerows (see Roads Act, Wildlife Act, above). However, in specific cases, hedgerows can be protected under the Planning and Development Act. These cases include Areas of Special Amenity and Landscape Conservation Orders, which can be designated by local authorities and within which certain exempt activities, such as hedgerow management, can be controlled. These two designated are very unlikely to be made on any significant scale for political reasons.

Local authorities can also make **Tree Preservation Orders (TPOs)**. Although no TPOs have been made in respect of hedgerows, it is conceivable that orders could be made for certain hedgerows of special historical or amenity importance.

European Communities (Environmental Impact Assessment) (Amendment) Regulations, 1999 (S.I. No. 93 of 1999), and Local Government (Planning and Development) Regulations, 1999 (S.I. No 431 of 1999).

Many developments, depending on their nature, scale, location and cumulative impacts, must be subjected to environmental impact assessment (EIA). EIAs for road construction are required under the Roads Act, 1993 (see

The laws protecting hedgerows in Britain and Northern Ireland

In Britain, it is against the law to remove most hedgerows. The law is designed to protect ancient and species-rich hedgerows as defined by the Hedgerows Regulations, 1997 (Statutory Instrument 1997 No. 1160). These regulations do not apply in Northern Ireland where there is no direct statutory protection of hedgerows. The Wildlife (Northern Ireland) Order, 1985 prohibits the intentional damage or destruction of wild bird nests, and thus hedgerow trimming is controlled indirectly.

For a more detailed explanation of the legal safeguards for hedgerows in England and Wales, and Northern Ireland, visit the website of the Royal Society for the Protection of Birds:

http://www.rspb.org.uk/countryside/advice/hedge_protection/index.asp

above). In the context of developments affecting hedgerows, the following are examples of the types of projects which must be subjected to EIA:

- Restructuring of rural land holdings, if the area exceeds 100 ha
- Land drainage projects exceeding 1,000 ha
- Initial afforestation projects of 50ha or more.
- Quarries exceeding 5 ha and all mining projects

- Wind farms with more than five turbines or which would generate a total output greater than 5 MW
- Industrial estates over 15 ha
- Urban development over 2ha in the case of a business district, 10 hectares in the case of other parts of a built-up area, and 20 hectares elsewhere.

Official policies

Policies are courses of action taken by the Government (or the European Union) on issues of importance.

The National Biodiversity Plan emphasises the importance of hedgerows as wildlife habitats. The Plan aims to review the options on regulation of hedgerow removal and produce guidelines on hedgerows and biodiversity. The Plan also aims to develop Guides to Best Practice with local authorities and other bodies to safeguard biodiversity.

At local government level, many **local authorities** are now adopting heritage plans, and sometimes these plans will include objectives to protect hedgerows. One example of this new approach is taken from Leitrim County Council's Heritage Plan. It aims to —

- Engage all stakeholders in the development and implementation of a Hedgerow Conservation Policy for the county
- Carry out hedgerow survey of Co. Leitrim
- Establish demonstration sites of best practice for hedgerow management along road schemes
- Provide training to local authority staff on hedgerow management

- Identify and establish protection mechanisms for hedgerows of significant ecological and historical value
- Continue to support the annual 'Golden Mile' competition.

Coillte has produced guidelines for staff on the treatment of hedgerows on forestry sites (see Bibliography). The following is an extract from this document.

- When replanting, keep back 5m from drop of crown of old trees along the hedgerow.
- If there are many hedgerows on site, select the best of them and leave sufficient space around those — better to leave 5 metres unplanted outside one hedgerow than 2 metres along 3 of them.
- The best hedgerows are the older ones, identified by having an earthen embankment, drains and old/mature trees.
- Consider restoring hedgerows after clearfell, i.e. old embankments that run through the forest.
- Allow open space along at least 5m either side and consider planting the embankment with native species such as blackthorn, hawthorn, ash or hazel.
- Include the hedgerow in the area fenced for forestry.

Schemes

The Rural Environment Protection Scheme (REPS)

The REPS was introduced in 1994 as an incentive scheme for farmers to conserve the environment and heritage on their farms. The Department of Agriculture and Food run this voluntary scheme. The scheme is available to in excess of 70% of Irish farmers. REPS is flexible enough to facilitate the voluntary participation of all farmers. Thirty eight per cent of Irish farmers have joined the REPS as of 2004, for which they receive a yearly payment. Those farmers who join must maintain the entire farm according to the rules of the scheme, the main elements of which include:

- Ensuring that the farmyard and fertiliser use does not contribute to water pollution
- Conservation of wildlife habitats (e.g. woodlands, wetlands, hedgerows)
- Conservation of archaeological and historical sites (e.g. ring forts, wells, lime kilns)
- Maintenance of farm and field boundaries (such as hedgerows)

Hedgerow management is one of the main measures of the REPS. Under Measure 5, farmers must conserve and maintain hedgerows in the interest of stock control, wildlife and scenic appearance. A wide range of treatments for hedgerows are set out in the REPS, depending on the type of hedgerow and its previous management. These measures are compulsory for REPS farmers.

Farmers can also choose to participate in two optional measures which involve more time and energy than periodic hedgerow trimming: REJUVENATION, which involves 'major surgery' including coppicing and laying; and NEW HEDGEROW ESTABLISHMENT, which means planting a new hedge from scratch. These techniques are described in Chapters 5 and 6 respectively.

The REPS is a complex scheme, which has many measures not directly relevant to this book. Full details of the REPS are available from the Department of Agriculture and Food, Johnstown Castle, Co. Wexford, and the web site:[http://www.agriculture.gov.ie/index.jsp?file=areasofi/reps3/reps3.xml].

Neighbourwood Scheme

The objective of the Neighbourwood Scheme is to encourage local community and local authority involvement in planting new woodland. The scheme was designed with woodland in urban and suburban situations in mind. Although hedgerows are not the focus of the scheme, they are mentioned as features which give protection to newly established woodland. Ideally, hedgerows, where they exist, should be incorporated or linked into the planting scheme. Grants and further information are available from the Forest Service, Department of Agriculture and Food, Johnstown Castle, Co. Wexford. Web site: [http://www.agriculture.gov.ie/forestry/publications/neighbour.pdf]

Native Woodland Scheme

The Native Woodland Scheme was designed to help restore and create native woodlands. There is a strong emphasis on nature conservation, and like the Neighbourwood Scheme, hedgerows are viewed as complementary to existing and new plantings. Web site: [http://www.agriculture.gov.ie/forestry/publications/woodland.pdf]

'The Golden Mile' competition

'The Golden Mile' is described in Chapter 6.

The rules for the competition are set out below.

Marks are allocated from 0–10 for each of 21 categories and a weighting system is applied to each. Categories include:

- Road aspects: Road safety for walkers and drivers. Drainage, road signage/markings, road verges, corners.
- Quality and mix of roadside vegetation (particularly native species).
- Appropriateness of management of hedgerows, verges, structures, etc.
- Quality, condition, and maintenance level of old houses, castles, farm and other buildings.
- Condition and design of field entrances and old gates, stone walls; bridges, etc.
- General tidiness and absence of litter.
- Tidiness of farmyards, businesses, and other premises.
- Condition inside gates and ditches as seen from the road.
- Does the area have a peaceful rural character? Is the area suitable for walking?
- Interpretative signage — condition and appropriateness.
- Evidence of community input.

Autumn colour in a roadside hedgerow. (Photo: Catherine Keena)

Appendix 1. Native and naturalised hedgerow species

Species	Characteristics	Sites
Whitethorn (Hawthorn, May tree) *Crataegus monogyna* **Irish name:** Sceach gheal	Ubiquitous hedging shrub. Tough and fast growing. Withstands hard cutting and laying. Displays great variation in flower hue at blossom time. Important source of pollen and nectar for invertebrates.	Widespread. Tolerant of most soils. Does not thrive at high elevations and cannot tolerate wet conditions. Susceptible to Fire Blight. Should not be planted near tree nurseries or commercial orchards.
Blackthorn (Sloe) *Prunus spinosa* **Irish name:** Draighean	Quick-growing, forming an impenetrable stockproof barrier when well-established. Suckers readily, so needs regular management. Good for filling gaps in hedgerows. Withstands hard cutting. The sloes are eaten by birds. Food plant of the Brown Hairstreak butterfly.	Widespread. Thrives on heavy and sandy soils. Salt tolerant, suitable for coastal and exposed sites.
Dog-rose *Rosa spp.* **Irish name:** Feirdhris	Blooms vary in colour from white to deep pink. The hips develop in autumn and are an important source of food for wild birds and mammals such as field mice.	Widespread. Typically found in long-established hedgerows.
Bramble (Blackberry, briar) *Rubus spp.* **Irish name:** Dris	Often provides extra stockproofing in a hedge, and colonises rapidly. Flowers and fruit are food for a wide range of wildlife. If left unchecked, will encroach into fields by means of tip rooting.	Widespread.
Crab apple *Malus sylvestris* **Irish name:** Crann fia-úll	Makes a good hedge, but less impenetrable than whitethorn or blackthorn, and should be mixed with other species. Fruits are smaller and less colourful than cultivated varieties.	Found in most counties but not common. Suited to free-draining fertile soils. Will not thrive in heavy, cold clays.
Wild pear *Pyrus pyraster* **Irish name:** Piorra fiáin	Spiny branches and very small fruits. Full-grown trees have distinctive, columnar shape and produce heavy white blossom.	Limited distribution. Wild trees restricted to some Munster counties.

Species	Characteristics	Sites
Wild plum or Damson *Prunus domestica* **Irish name:** Baláiste	Introduced. The fruits are similar in shape and size to blackthorn sloes but purple in colour.	Can be found in many counties but uncommon.
Wild cherry *Prunus avium* **Irish name:** Crann Silín Fiáin	Brilliant white flowers in spring produce small, dark red, hanging cherries, eagerly eatern by birds.	Found in most counties.
Hazel *Corylus avellana* **Irish name:** Coll	Suitable for coppicing and laying. High amenity and wildlife value. Important early source of pollen for bees. Coppiced stems have many uses.	Widespread. Grows well on loams and mildly acid soils. Not tolerant of wet situations. Good choice for free draining, limestone soils.
Holly *Ilex aquifolium* **Irish name:** Cuileann	Slow-growing evergreen, forming a tough, stockproof barrier. Good for filling gaps in hedgerows. Susceptible to frost damage. Food plant of the Holly Blue butterfly.	Widespread. Will grow on dry soils, sands and gravel. Shade-tolerant. Will not grow on wet sites. Both male and female plants are required to produce berries.
Gorse (Furze or Whin) *Ulex europaeus* **Irish name:** Aiteann gallda	Abundant in drier parts of Ireland. Does not form a good stockproof barrier on its own. Should be cut back hard when 'leggy' and thin at the base. Gorse should be trimmed in late winter. Supports many insects and spiders, which birds feed on in turn. Also gives good shelter for nesting birds.	Widespread. Does well on poor, light soils. Will grow on very dry and exposed sites where other species cannot thrive. Salt-tolerant and suitable for coastal and exposed sites.
Willow *Salix species* **Irish name:** Saileach	The many species are sometimes difficult to identify and hybridise readily. Very fast-growing. Suitable for laying. Willows make poor stockproof hedges. Male catkins are an early source of pollen for bees.	Useful for wet sites where species choice is limited. Will tolerate flooding. Can be propagated from hardwood cuttings.
Wych elm *Ulmus glabra* **Irish name:** Leamhán sléibhe	The name 'wych' means pliant. Virtually absent as a mature tree, due to the ravages of Dutch Elm Disease. The leaves can sometimes be confused with hazel, but are thinner and the leaf blades bulge at the base on one side than the other.	Widespread, but now only as saplings in hedgerows.

Species	Characteristics	Sites
Elder *Sambucus nigra* **Irish name:** Trom	Common hedgerow shrub with greyish, corky bark and branches containing a soft pith. The sprays of white flowers are followed by bunches of dark purple elderberries. Flower s and fruit provide food for a wide range of wildlife species.	Widespread. Seeds dispersed by birds, which eat the fruit. Grows in most soils.
Guelder Rose *Viburnum opulus* **Irish name:** Caor chon	Handsome hedgerow shrub with lobed maple-like leaves which colour richly in autumn. The discs of creamy blossom in June in June and July produce translucent crimson fruits which are eaten by birds.	Widespread. Often found in new roadside planting schemes. Likes moist soils and is often found near drains.
Honeysuckle (Woodbine) *Lonicera periclymenum* **Irish name:** Féithleann	Common, woody climber. The fragrant flowers attract moths and other insects and are followed by bright red berries readily eaten by birds.	Widespread.
Spindle (Pegwood) *Euonymus europaeus* **Irish name:** Feoras	Vigorous, green stemmed small tree also found in hedgerows. The hard wood was used in former times to make wooden spindles, and clothes pegs. The small greenish flowers produce scarlet 4-lobed seed capsules, called 'cardinals' hats'. The fruits are eaten and dispersed by birds that pass the orange seeds after eating them.	Widespread but more common in limestone areas of the Midlands.
Buckthorn *Rhamnus catharticus* **Irish name:** Paide bréan	Food plant of Brimstone butterfly. The small, greenish-yellow flowers appear in clusters and produce a small, fleshy black fruit. The specific name 'catharticus' derives from its powerful purgative and diuretic qualities.	Uncommon. Prefers lime-rich soils. Found around the shores of Upper Lough Erne and the Shannon.
Alder buckthorn *Frangula alnus* **Irish name:** Draighean fearna	Food plant of Brimstone butterfly.	Once common, but now only moderately distributed. Less common in south. Can be found around the shores of Lough Ree. Likes moist sites.

Species	Characteristics	Sites
Clematis (Traveller's-joy, Old Man's Beard) *Clematis vitalba* **Irish name:** Geabhrán	Climbing shrub which often takes over hedgerows. The small, greenish-cream flowers attract bees and flies. The masses of feathery fruits, so conspicuous in autumn and winter, give this plant its colloquial name 'Old Man's Beard'. Beautiful shrub of the autumn hedgerow and particularly after overnight frost.	Widespread. Thrives in lime-rich soils.
Dogwood *Cornus sanguinea* **Irish name:** Conbhaiscne	Conspicuous, straight red stems in winter. Leaves turn dark red in autumn. The white flowers, their scent resembling whitethorn, produce black fruits in autumn. Dogwood roots readily from hardwood cuttings planted in autumn.	Found in most counties. Common on lime-rich soils.
Wild privet *Ligustrum vulgare* **Irish name:** Pribhéad	Medium sized shrub, partially evergreen. Closely related to *Ligustrum ovalifolium*, a Japanese import found in gardens throughout Ireland. The heavily-scented, white flowers produce small black berries.	Widespread but considered native only in Limerick, Clare, North Tipperary and Dublin. Prefers dry, lime-rich soils.
Ash *Fraxinus excelsior* **Irish name:** Fuinseog	Usually the last native tree to come into leaf and the first to shed its leaves in autumn. The fruits are large, flat 'keys' which are wind-dispersed. The large, black buds are very noticeable in winter.	Widespread. Demands good soil conditions, preferably sheltered, moist, well-drained loams.
Ivy *Hedera helix* **Irish name:** Eidhnéan	Self-supporting climber. Pale yellow flowers emerge in winter, and the berries ripen in spring, food for blackbirds and thrushes. Opinions on the benefits or disadvantages of ivy vary.	Widespread.

Sources: *Our Trees; Specifications for REPS Planners in the preparation of REPS 3 plans* (see Bibliography).

Appendix 2. Hedgerows, houses and planning

Local authorities can play their part in the conservation of hedgerows, through the planning process. Some local authorities have adopted progressive policies for hedgerow management and protection in their County Development Plans. Development plans must be reviewed every six years and public submissions are invited during the time that the draft plan is on public display. Local authorities are becoming increasingly conscious of the need to protect the natural heritage, but they will need to be encouraged to adopt policies that make a real difference in practice. If you would like to see better conservation policies for hedgerows, especially in relation to house building and road development, you should make a submission to your local authority.

Below are extracts from the South Tipperary County Development Plan 2003, illustrating how one local authority is acting to protect hedgerows in the rural landscape.

CHAPTER 5. HOUSING
Policy HSG 5: Rural Clusters
Policy HSG 5 is designed to provide a more sustainable option to single houses dotted along the roadside. Developments considered under this policy must be set in a well-landscaped setting, and should integrate well with existing hedgerows and landscape features.

POLICY HSG 8: RURAL HOUSING IN THE OPEN COUNTRYSIDE
Applicants that meet the criteria set out in Policy HSG 8 must maintain existing hedgerows.

POLICY HSG.9: RURAL HOUSING IN PRESSURE AREAS
Housing granted under policy HSG.9 shall conform to 'Guidelines for Rural Housing' and must, inter alia, maintain existing hedgerows, and the land between the roadside and the houses must be planted with trees as set out in the guidelines.

POLICY HSG 10: SPECIAL HOUSING POLICY
It is the policy of the Council to provide for new housing in areas subject to significant decline, provided, inter alia, that existing hedgerows are maintained.4

CHAPTER 8. DESIGN GUIDELINES AND GENERAL STANDARDS
8.4.1 Residential Development in Open Countryside

Among the design guidelines and general standards for residential development in the open countryside, the Council stipulates the following:

Boundary-landscape treatment: Double rows of hedging (holly, hawthorn, blackthorn, field maple). Hardwood trees, of those native species already occurring in the vicinity of the development, shall be planted every 5m within the hedge (field maple, sycamore, silver birch, rowan, whitebeam). All planting to take place in the season following occupation.

Roadside Boundary: The existing hedgerow shall be maintained, where, in the opinion of the Council, there is no conflict with the requirements of the Council for the provision of improved carriageway widths, except at the entrance, and supplemented where necessary.

Land between site and roadside: This area shall be planted with trees, 50% being hardwoods, where, in the opinion of the Council, there is no conflict with road maintenance requirements.

Existing trees and hedgerows are also required to be protected in industrial and agricultural development.

APPENDIX 2. GUIDELINES FOR RURAL HOUSING

3. Locating a house in the countryside

Buildings in the countryside alter and influence the landscape profoundly and become focal points for the eye. Thus, it is essential that buildings are located so that they can be readily assimilated into the landscape. Houses must be treated as objects in the landscape and due weight attached to their siting and form accordingly. The site selection process is a critical determinant of the visual impact and energy efficiency of the dwelling. A holistic approach should be adopted in the site selection process, displaying sensitivity towards the rural environment and natural energy conservation.

3.6. Shelter Planting

Ireland has a higher average wind speed than most European countries and consequently, substantial shelter planting is required to counteract the severe climatic conditions experienced in many rural locations. Manicured suburban type gardens commonly found in rural areas do not provide sufficient climatic protection. Shelter planting may be difficult to establish in exposed areas, yet it is vital to create wind free zones around the house and associated buildings.

Trees shelter buildings from cold winds and driving rain, thereby potentially reducing domestic fuel consumption by 20 per cent. Privacy and improved appearance of the immediate environment as a place to live and work are further benefits that may be derived from shelter planting. Aesthetically, shelter planting may soften hard outlines, harmonise new buildings with their surrounds and reduce their dominance in the rural landscape.

The following factors should be taken into account in the provision of successful shelter planting:

- Retain existing Trees and Hedgerows
- Consider pre-planting
- Shelter planting should be across the path of the wind
- Hedging is preferable to concrete walls as boundary treatment and as a good shelterbelt
- A shelterbelt should consist of not less than

three rows of trees with a row of broadleaved trees included together with a hedge.
- Hedges for stock proof purposes should consist solely of hawthorn, whilst in very exposed conditions planting should be positioned on the leeward side of a stonewall, dyke or timber lath screen.
- Native deciduous trees are preferable to coniferous on amenity grounds and are advantageous in that they provide shade from excessive sun in the summer and allow sunlight through in the winter.

6. Boundary treatment

Simple treatment of the boundary and entry to the dwelling yields the most successful results. Existing boundaries and hedgerows should be retained where possible to help root new buildings more naturally in the landscape. The conservation of existing stonewalls, mature trees and hedgerows serve to nestle the building in the landscape, making it less conspicuous. The use of natural stone walls where used locally is preferable to plastered blockwork to ensure continuity of form throughout the landscape. Avoid the use of brick and timber clad fencing which are not appropriate for the rural environment, rendering a 'suburban feel' to the open countryside.

Access roads must be designed to follow the contours of the land and meander across the gradient. Avoid access roads that follow a direct line between the entrance and dwelling, resulting in a stark unnatural gash in the landscape. To guard against a harsh visual outcome, access roads should take account of site topography and should comprise of gravel or shale rather than macadam.

Appendix 3. Further information and contacts

Networks for Nature (NfN), PO Box 9184 Churchtown, Dublin 14. Tel: 087 6893329 Email: info@networksfornature.com

Professional Agricultural Contractors of Ireland (PAC), PO Box 9, Athlone, Co. Westmeath Tel: 090 6437518. Email: info@pacireland.com

Agriculture
Information on the REPS and other agricultural schemes can be obtained from the Department of Agriculture and Food, Johnstown Castle, Co. Wexford. www.agriculture.gov.ie

Teagasc advisory and information material can be obtained from local Teagasc offices. Contact Teagasc HQ, Oak Park, Carlow. Tel: 059 9170200 Colleges offering Hedgerow Management and Mechanical Hedgecutting Courses:
Ballyhaise, Co. Cavan 049 4338108
Gurteen, Co. Tipperary 067 21282
Pallaskenry, Co. Limerick 067 393100
Kildalton, Co. Kilkenny 051 643105
www.teagasc.ie

The Irish Farmers Association can be contacted at Irish Farm Centre, Bluebell, Dublin 12.
Tel: +353-1-4500266. www.ifa.ie

Trees and Forestry
Information on forestry policy, legislation and schemes can be obtained from the Forest Service, Department of Agriculture and Food, Johnstown Castle, Co. Wexford. www.agriculture.gov.ie

Coillte, the State Forestry Board, which manages the public forest estate, can be contacted at: Coillte Teoranta, Newtownmountkennedy, Co. Wicklow. Tel: +353-1-2011111. www.coillte.ie

Crann, a voluntary organisation devoted to planting broadleaf trees, can be contacted at: Crann, Crank House, Main Street, Banagher, County Offaly. Tel: +353-1-509 51718. E-mail: info@crann.ie www.crann.ie

The Tree Council of Ireland is a voluntary organisation which promotes the conservation, maintenance and planting of trees. Contact: The Tree Council of Ireland, The Park, Cabinteely, Dublin 18. Tel: +353-1-2849211.
E-mail: rees@treecouncil.ie
www.treecouncil.ie

Hedge Laying Association of Ireland Contact the Secretary, Moyvore, Mullingar, Co. Westmeath. Tel: 087 2794045 Email: hlai@eircom.net

Wildlife
The National Parks and Wildlife Service of the Department of Environment, Heritage and Local Government can be contacted at 7 Ely Place Dublin 2. Tel. +353-1-6472300; LoCall 1890 321 421. E-mail natureconservation@environ.ie www.duchas.ie

Birdwatch Ireland is a voluntary organisation dedicated to the conservation of Ireland's wild birds and their habitats. Contact: Birdwatch Ireland, Rockingham House, Newcastle, Co. Wicklow. Tel: 353-1-2819878. www.birdwatchireland.ie

The Irish Wildlife Trust is a voluntary organisation dedicated to the conservation of Ireland's wildlife and habitats. Contact: Irish Wildlife Trust, 21 Northumberland Road, Dublin 4. Tel: +353-1-6604530. E-mail: iwt@eircom.net www.iwt.ie

Heritage
The Heritage Council, the statutory advisory body on all aspects of Ireland's heritage, can be contacted at Rothe House, Kilkenny. Tel: +353-56-7770777. E-mail: mail@heritagecouncil.ie www.heritagecouncil.ie

An Taisce, a voluntary organisation dedicated to protecting all aspects of Ireland's heritage, can be contacted at The Tailors' Hall, Back Lane, Dublin 8. Tel: +353-1-4541786. E-mail: info@antaisce.org www.antaisce.org

Further Education and Training Awards Council
(FETAC) East Point Plaza, East Point Business Pk, Dublin 3. Tel: +353-1- 865 9500
Email: information@fetac.ie

Legislation
The full text of the national legislation listed in Chapter 10 can be obtained from the Government Publications Office, Molesworth St., Dublin 2 or by visiting the web site: www.irishstatutebook.ie

EU environmental legislation can be obtained from the European Commission, European House, Dublin 2 or from the EU web site:
http://europa.eu.int/comm/environment

Bibliography

Chapter 1.

Feehan, John (2003). *Farming in Ireland: History, Heritage and Environment*. University College Dublin, Faculty of Agriculture.

Joyce, P.W (1971). *A Social History of Ireland*. M.H. Gill.

Long, Harry (no date). Settlement and Social Life in Feagh McHugh O'Byrne's Ballinacor. Web address: http://homepage.tinet.ie/~nobyrne/Settlement_in_Feagh_OByrne_Ballinacor.htm

Mac Coitir, Niall (2003) *Irish Trees: Myths, Legends and Folklore*. The Collins Press, Cork. ISBN: 1-903464-33-1.

Memory Patterson, Jaqueline (1996) *Tree Wisdom: The definitive guidebook to the myth, folklore and healing power of trees*. Thorsons, London. ISBN: 0-7225-3408-6

Mitchell, Frank (1986). *The Shell Guide to Reading the Irish Landscape*. Michael Joseph/Country House.

Young, Arthur (1970). *A tour of Ireland, with general observation of the present state of that kingdom: 1776-1779, Vols 1-2*. Edited by A.W. Hutton. Irish University Press.

Chapter 2.

Aalen, F.H.A, Whelan, Kevin and Matthew Stout, Eds. (1997). *Atlas of the Irish Rural Landscape*. Cork University Press.

Feehan, John (2003). *Farming in Ireland: History, Heritage and Environment*. University College Dublin, Faculty of Agriculture.

Hickie, D. A (1985). A hedge study of North County Dublin. Trinity College Dublin, University thesis. Unpublished.

Hickie, D., Smyth, E., Bohnsack, U., Scott. S., and Baldock, D (1999) *Impacts of agriculture schemes and payments on aspects of Ireland's heritage*. A report for the Heritage Council. Kilkenny.

Lewis, Samuel (1837). *A Topographical Dictionary of Ireland*. London.

McCracken, Eileen (1971). *Irish Woods Since Tudor Times*. David and Charles, 1971.

Young, Arthur (1970). *A tour of Ireland, with general observation of the present state of that kingdom: 1776-1779, Vols 1-2*. Edited by A.W. Hutton. Irish University Press.

Chapter 3.

Feehan, J (2001). The impact of the Rural Environment Protection Scheme (REPS) on the diversity of flora and carabidae fauna within the Republic of Ireland. Trinity College Dublin PhD thesis. Unpublished.

Flynn, M (2002). An investigation of the relationship between avian biodiversity and hedgerow management as prescribed under the Irish Rural Environment Protection Scheme. Royal College of Surgeons in Ireland PhD thesis. Unpublished.

Irish Wildlife Federation (1987). Irish Hedgerow Survey: Report No. 1. Structure and Wildlife. *Supplement to the Badger* 7 Spring 1987.

Keena, C (1998). A study of hedgerows on thirty farms participating in the Rural Environment Protection Scheme in County Cavan. UCD thesis. Unpublished.

Kenny, K (2004). The farmer and the hedgerow – Farmer attitudes and woody species composition of hedgerows in the Castlerea district of County Roscommon. UCD thesis. Unpublished

Northern Ireland Habitat Action Plan: Species-rich hedgerows. Final Draft, April 2003. Web address: http://www.ehsni.gov.uk/pubs/publications/Hedgerow_Web_Version_April_03.pdf

Lysaght, L (1990). An investigation of habitat selection in hedgerow nesting birds in mid West

Ireland. PhD Thesis. Department of Geography, Trinity College, Dublin.

People's Millennium Forests (2000). *Our Trees: A guide to growing Ireland's native trees in celebration of a new Millennium.* The People's Millennium Forests Project. ISBN: 0-9518612-5-5

Pilcher, Jonathan, and Valerie Hall (2001). *Flora Hibernica: The wild flowers, plants and trees of Ireland.* The Collins Press, Cork. ISBN: 1-903464-03-X

Pointereau, P., Steiner, C., de Miguel, E., and D. Hickie (2000). *Trees, Hedges and Water.* Solagro, Toulouse.

Chapter 5
Teagasc Information Leaflets: The Value of Hedgerows; Routine Trimming of Hedgerows; Hedgerow Rejuvenation. Teagasc Offices.

Chapter 6
Curtis, T.G.F., and H.N. McGough (1988). *The Irish Red Data Book: 1. Vascular Plants.* Stationery Office, Dublin. ISBN: 0-7076-0032-4

Moriarty, Christopher (1994). *By-Ways Rather Than Highways: Exploring Ireland's Hidden Places: 38 Routes to Discover by Car.* Wolfhound Press. ISBN: 0863273734

Chapter 7
Maclean, Murray (1992). *New Hedges for the Countryside.* Farming Press Books, United Kingdom. ISBN: 0-85236-242-0 5

Teagasc Information Leaflet: New Farm Hedgerows.

Chapter 10.
Department of Arts, Heritage, Gaeltacht and the Islands (2002). *National Biodiversity Plan.* Stationery Office, Dublin. ISBN: 0-7557-1328-1

Coillte Draft Training Manual (2001). Environmental Impact Appraisal, Protection & Enhancement: A Training Course Manual for the appraisal of environmental impacts on forestry operations sites. Internal document. Unpublished.

Appendix 1.
Scannell, Mary J.P., and Synott, Donal M (1987). *Census Catalogue of the Flora of Ireland.* The Stationery Office, Dublin.

The People's Millenniun Forests Project (2000). *Our Trees.* The People's Millenium Forests Project, Ireland.